HUMILITY
a practical approach

BY COMMON CONSENT PRESS is a non-profit publisher dedicated to producing affordable, high-quality books that help define and shape the Latter-day Saint experience. BCC Press publishes books that address all aspects of Mormon life. Our mission includes finding manuscripts that will contribute to the lives of thoughtful Latter-day Saints, mentoring authors and nurturing projects to completion, and distributing important books to the Mormon audience at the lowest possible cost.

HUMILITY

A PRACTICAL APPROACH

SHAWN TUCKER

For information contact
By Common Consent Press
4900 Penrose Dr.
Newburgh, IN 47630

Cover design: D Christian Harrison
Book design: Andrew Heiss

www.bccpress.org
ISBN-13: 978-1-948218-45-0

10 9 8 7 6 5 4 3 2 1

For Tina Marie, Sprite, Brycie Brycie Bear, My G, and Nicole

CONTENTS

INTRODUCTION

Since twins are considered evil and taboo, the common community practice is to leave newborns out to die. The sound of those abandoned children causes confusion and pain for one young man in the village. This young man's father, a well-respected village leader, is demanding, emotionally distant, and deeply disappointed in his son. In order for that father to save face in the community, he brutally murdered a young man who was like an adopted son and brother. These painful situations—the deaths of twins born in the village, his conflicts with his father, and his brother Ikemefuna's ruthless murder—leave him feeling lost, confused, and alone.

In the midst of this painful loneliness and confusion Nwoye, a character in Chinua Achebe's novel *Things Fall Apart*, hears the poetry and the music of Christian missionaries. Nwoye does not understand the poetry, the music, or what is being taught. The poetry of this new religion, for Nwoye, was "something felt in the marrow." The narrator explains what it was about the poetry and the new religion that had such an impact on Nwoye: "the hymn about brothers who sat in darkness and in fear seemed to answer a vague and persistent question that haunted his young soul—the question of the twins crying in the bush and the question of Ikemefuna who was killed." The narrator finishes by saying, "He felt a relief within as the hymn poured into his parched soul. The words of the hymn were like the drops of frozen rain melting on the dry palate of the panting earth."

I start with this little example because it describes one aspect of humility. Nwoye's parched soul and the dry palate of the panting earth demonstrate humility's sense of longing and need. But longing and need are only one aspect of humility. To understand humility's many sides, we will listen to a wide variety of stories. There are stories of everyday members of the Church of Jesus Christ of Latter-day Saints along with insights from church leaders past and present. There is a story that Plato told about love as well as examples from *Moby Dick*, *Jane Eyre*, and *King Lear*. There are insights from a Harvard-trained therapist and from the ceramics instructor at the small, private university where I work. We will hear ideas from people like Alma and Mormon and C.S. Lewis, but we will also examine a gigantic foam finger in sacrament meeting and an ironically dark conspiracy involving light bulbs. We will talk about new missionaries and experienced missionaries, about cilantro, about tacos at a ward potluck, and about mastodon hunters. These stories will give you a clearer picture of what it means to be humble in your relationship with God and in your relationships with others. We will examine principles like meekness, vulnerability, seeing your weaknesses, respect, and modesty, as well as enmity, self-righteousness, willful blindness, hypocrisy, and pride. What comes to light is how humility is helping you to become complete, whole, and fully formed into the person that your Heavenly Parents want you to be. As you see humility with greater clarity, you will see ways to continue to draw on the unique blessings that humility provides. You might see ways to be more humble. Studying humility explains the role of humility's longing and need. Those longings and needs are like a dry, parched soul, and this study can lead you to the gracious gift of God's rain.

HUMILITY
IN YOUR
RELATIONSHIP
WITH GOD

YOU ARE THE 1
LORD MY GOD

GREG, GIVING UP

When I watch the video today, my first thought is how big his
head is. When he was alive, yes, he had a large head, but it was
well suited to the body of a tall and broad-shouldered young
man. It also matched his large personality. But in the video, the
camera seems like it might be a little too close. I don't know who
was in charge of camera placement, and I don't think I was there.
Maybe the head looks so large because they didn't want to show
his bed, all of the medicine he was taking, or how much thinner
and weaker his body had become. They wanted whoever would
watch this final interview to see Greg's face. They wanted to cap-
ture his voice and his eyes before he was gone. They wanted to
give him one last chance to offer his testimony and to express his
love for his family and the Lord.

The video would have been shot in 1986, sometime before

March 19th. During the summer of the previous year, Greg broke his leg. He was home from college, getting money together to go on a mission. It was when the broken leg was examined that doctors found the bone cancer. The next eight or nine months were the slow process of giving up. First Greg gave up playing basketball. He loved to play, and I remember him shooting around and coaching our church basketball team, but the cancer prevented him from actually running around on the court with us. With the medical treatment came more things he had to give up, like his hair and some of the food he loved. He wanted to leave for his mission by his birthday in November and then by Christmas, but he had to give that up. There was some giving up of friends, young people who were seventeen, eighteen, nineteen-year-olds who could not deal with this situation. This was followed by the big giving ups: giving up hope for speedy remission, giving up hope for a delayed recovery, and then giving up hope for any recovery at all.

I was seventeen when my then nineteen-year-old friend Greg Willis died from bone cancer. When I watch the video made toward the end of his life, besides noting how big his head looks on the screen, I also recall something important about him: he loved God and was willing to submit to whatever God had for him. From the start, Greg was willing to give up a few things, and then he was willing to give up more things, and then he gave up everything. Greg was a great young man—friendly, outgoing, kind to everyone. He wanted to be a missionary and eventually a husband and father. He held tenaciously to his hope and faith that God could heal him, but that blessing never came. In the process of giving all of that up, Greg turned to God in love and humility.

Greg was remarkable, but not out-of-the-ordinary. I believe that you, like all of us, have passed, are probably passing, and will pass through painful experiences that push you to the limits of your faith and humility. Loss, reversals, nasty surprises or disappointments, irony, or blessings that come too slowly, or don't come at all, force you to decide if you will trust and submit to God or not. Maybe you submit willingly and quickly. Greg seemed to do that. He did not know why he was dying, but he trusted in loving Heavenly Parents and in Their promises for him and for his loved ones.

I'm guessing that you have seen similar submission. You may have seen someone like Greg, someone whose faith, testimony, and love give them power to submit to God. You may have had chances, difficult chances, to submit to God in your own life. If you have not yet, don't worry, you will. God will ask you to give things up, things that are very important to you. The willingness to submit in faith and love to God, the willingness to say with your whole being, "You are the Lord my God," the willingness to let God take in spite of pain or pleadings or promises, that willingness is humility.

JERILYN, YES YOU CAN

Jerilyn loves to tell her story. When I called to ask her about her experiences, she jumped right in. The story starts when she was living in Oregon and thoroughly enjoying life there. It was there that she got more and more involved in work that she found very spiritually satisfying. It was a work that she describes as binding up the wounds of injured saints. When I heard Jerilyn Hassell Poole's voice, I was moved by how valuable this work is to her and how precious those souls are. Like the best church service, Jerilyn has moments when she feels like she gets to be the hands that God uses to bless the lives of others. Jerilyn has felt called to serve a very particular group of church members, specifically lesbian, gay, bisexual, queer, and transgender members of the Church of Jesus Christ of Latter-day Saints. In Oregon she opened her home as a place for those church members to feel safe over Christmas. In Oregon she also connected with many more struggling saints living in Utah. As those people reached out to her, she wanted to offer more support to them.

When she looks back on this experience now, she sees God's hand guiding her to Utah. The house she was renting in Oregon was being sold by the landlord, and she could not find anywhere to live. At that time, a friend in Provo had just bought a house that she wanted to rent out. That friend contacted Jerilyn in the hope that she might want to rent it. She told Jerilyn that she was in the top five of people that she could ever imagine renting the house to. Picking up the family and moving to a different state, especially to a place where she knew that she would find many challenges, was a very difficult decision to make. Jerilyn sought God's help in making this decision. Just before the family was to move to Utah, an alternative home in Oregon became available.

She reconsidered moving to Utah, but every time she thought of not going to Utah her mind went completely blank. She took this "stupor of thought" as a message that she should indeed move to Utah. When she still vacillated over this decision, she felt a powerful manifestation from the Lord prompting her to move.

Jerilyn wanted God's reassurance that moving to Utah was the right decision. She wanted to know that the Lord would be with her and with her loved ones. She felt God's reassurance, and that reassurance brought an encouragement that was difficult to believe. It was difficult to believe in part because she knew of the challenges that she would face in Utah. But it was also difficult to believe because it seemed too good to be true. Jerilyn wanted to help the members of the church that she felt called to serve. Living in Provo would give her many more opportunities. With God's reassurance, Jerilyn and her family moved, and in the years that they have spent in Provo, they have been instrumental in blessing and literally saving the lives of many, many people. At the end of my conversation with Jerilyn, she told me that she loves to share her story because it highlights how God takes care of each of God's children.

Maybe you have had an experience like this. Maybe the Lord has said, "Yes, you can do this thing that seems exciting and challenging." Maybe the Lord has said, "Yes, you can go to that school," or "Yes, you can marry that person" or "Yes, you can pursue that career." The reassurance is powerful because it just seems too good to be true. Or maybe the Lord told you that you don't have to go to that school, marry that person, or pursue that career. Perhaps God reassured you that you will get married or comforted you that you will not have to marry. Maybe God told you that you can stay home with your kids, or maybe the Lord reassured you that you don't have to stay home with your kids. God may have said, as a pleasant, joyous surprise, that yes, you can have a child or another child, or perhaps God said, as an equally pleasant and joyous surprise, that you don't have to have any more children or any children at all. God may have quietly yet powerfully reassured you that yes, you can make your marriage work, or God may have given you an equally powerful confidence that you do not need to stay with a harmful spouse or in a toxic relationship. Saying with your whole being "You are the Lord my God" to God's good news and encouragement is just as much a part of humility as trusting God when you are asked to sacrifice or to give something up.

MARTY, GOD IS NOT ENOUGH

Marty wasn't sure if he wanted to talk with me about his experiences. He is not particularly private, but he didn't want to hurt any of the people he loves, so I agreed to change Marty's name and some of the unimportant particulars of his story.

Marty thought his problem was behind him. After his mission he thought it was over. After he got married, he thought it was over. After his first child, and then second child, and then after some church callings—after all of these life-changing events, Marty thought that the seemingly irresistible pull of pornography could finally be resisted.

But it could not be resisted. Marty was starting to feel hopeless. He went through a time when he was fasting and praying every Sunday, begging the Lord to forgive and to free him, offering a broken heart and contrite spirit but then falling right back into his problem by Wednesday or Thursday. This was a particularly dark time. He was humble, willing to submit to God, and yet he still found himself powerless in the face of his struggles.

It was around that time that Marty was told in a blessing his bishop gave him to "seek knowledge." He had already read several books for LDS and non-LDS audiences about dealing with compulsive pornography use, but he followed the counsel and sought wisdom. He reached out to respected professionals. He learned about treatments like Acceptance and Commitment Therapy, and that approach was well suited to Marty's personality. He learned about mindfulness and the benefits of meditation, all of which gave him some of the knowledge his inspired bishop had told him to seek.

He decided to attend the Addiction Recovery Program. It wasn't just the shame and embarrassment that had kept him from going to ARP meetings earlier. He had studied the manual, and it all just seemed like an elaboration on the repentance process. He knew how to repent, and he didn't think he needed a program to do that. He told me that different people get different things from the program, but the most important thing he found in the Addiction Recovery Program meetings was compassion. The people in those meetings knew the worst and most embarrassing things about him, but they extended compassion to him.

And it was there that Marty also had a chance to extend compassion. He could get text messages during the week from people who were struggling. He could text them back some encouraging words. He could pray for them. He could also text them when he needed help, encouragement, or a prayer. He felt buoyed up by them. That compassion was an essential element for Marty in dealing with the otherwise overwhelming power that pornography had in his life.

Marty was humble. He was willing to say with his whole soul, "You are the Lord my God" even before therapy, meditation, and the Addiction Recovery Program. But in spite of that humility, God did not take away his struggle. "I don't know if this fits your book," Marty told me, "but one day I concluded that God was not enough." When I asked what Marty meant by that, he said that his problems required more than faith and humility. His problem required other people. Marty said that the people he could text when he was struggling or the professionals who taught him how to not be swept away by waves of craving were essential to his recovery. Marty learned to say to God, "You are the Lord my God, but sometimes we, Your children, need each other to do Your work."

Have you had experiences like this, times when important answers or strength did not come? Perhaps you have done all you can and still not received the promised blessings. Humility can mean waiting on the Lord and on yourself, giving God time to turn your weakness to strength. Humility can also mean reaching out to others. Perhaps you have had God work in your life through others, through a parent, a sibling, a teacher, a coach, a boss, a therapist or other professional, or a church leader. Perhaps you have been there for another, offering insights or extending compassion. Perhaps you have been there so that others could receive essential help or blessings that would not come otherwise. God's work is collaborative, and, with complete devotion to God, we all need each other and we all get to participate.

BRETT, GOD DOESN'T CARE, SORT OF

What I picture is someone like Enos who prayed all day until the Lord answered his prayer. Only Brett, apparently, didn't last that long. Still, he held out most of the day, which is much longer than I would have lasted. Brett had taken his bike to a quiet place out of town. There, he waited patiently, willing to hear and follow whatever the Lord told him. He had his scriptures. He had a notebook and a pen. He was ready for the answer. There he was. Waiting for the answer. And he didn't stop waiting for his answer until a good part of the day had passed. But even then, still no answer.

What happened next was what sounds like some fairly angry peddling back home, frustrated with God's unwillingness to tell Brett which law school the Lord wanted him to attend. Was God testing his patience? Was he out of tune with the Lord? Surely the Lord would not leave such an important decision to mere chance, and Brett was humbly willing to receive and act upon God's direction. That is, of course, until no direction came.

It was while peddling home that Brett Scharffs explains

that with the cadence of his peddling came the increasingly persistent thought: "Honor your priesthood and remember your covenants." With each up-and-down of the peddles the two principals were repeated and reinforced. It was then that Brett got his answer—that God didn't care where he attended law school but that, wherever he attended, God wanted him to honor his priesthood and remember his covenants.

Brett Scharffs' experience, an experience he shared in his 2005 BYU devotional "The Most Important Three Things in the World," further illustrates the idea of humility as submission to God. Submitting to God can mean giving up, as happened with Greg, and it can mean getting reassurance and encouragement to do something wonderful, as happened to Jerilyn. Submission means understanding how God uses you and uses others to do God's work. Submission can also include distinguishing what God leaves up to you. Submission can mean learning to make certain decisions, even important ones, without divine command. In Brett Scharffs' example, he had not initially considered that God would not direct him in this issue, but he was willing to receive the unexpected answer. God wanted him to attend the law school of his choice. While he was in law school and then throughout his life, God wanted Brett to honor the priesthood and live by his covenants.

Humility is complete submission, commitment, and devotion to God. Humility is saying, with your whole being, "You are the Lord my God." This humility gives you power to trust even when God takes away. Greg humbly trusted even when God took away. Humility helps you believe when God reassures you of something that might seem too good to be true. Jerilyn believed God when God's message was reassuring and joyous. Humility provides hope when God does not immediately answer or when God answers your prayers through others, as happened with Marty. Humility gives you wisdom to discern what is God's role and what is yours, as Brett learned.

So, if humility gives such power, hope, and wisdom, how can we develop humility? To explain this, in the next chapter I will talk about a whale and about friendship.

know God merely by studying what language, literature, religion, art, or science might tell you about the Lord. You must find God. Greg, Jerilyn, Marty, and Brett could submit to God, could be completely committed and devoted to God, because they had experiences with God.

THE HARROW AND THE SLOW BURN

When I had read these Book of Mormon verses in the past, I had never really paid attention to words like "harrow" or "rack." In Elder Packer's April 2001 General Conference talk "The Touch of the Master's Hand," he explains that a harrow is a frame with spikes on it, a farm tool used to rip and break up the soil. A rack is a torture device. Alma the Younger uses these words to describe how he felt when he experienced the pain and guilt his sins caused him. In verse 12 of Alma 36, he tells his son Helaman, "I was racked with eternal torment, for my soul was harrowed up to the greatest degree and racked with all of my sins." It was in the midst of this torture that Alma remembered hearing about "the coming of one Jesus Christ," and, as you recall, when he cried in his heart to experience the mercy Christ offers, he experienced that mercy.

Alma the Younger's experience with God was an experience of God's atoning power, God's power to take sins away. I believe that repentance and forgiveness are the central and fundamental way that all of us experience God. Out in the stormy seas of excruciating guilt and brokenness, in the heart of this greatest peril, we find God, but instead of angry flukes, we find peace, mercy, and compassion.

You may or may not have had an experience as dramatic as Alma the Younger's, but your experience of having the faith sufficient to repent brought you one of the most important experiences with God. When I have seen how my sins have harmed the people I love, have harmed me, and how they have caused pain to the God who loves all of us, and then when I have felt those sins forgiven and felt God's love spread out to heal, I have experienced firsthand God's power. That experience gives me faith. That faith helps me hope, believe, and submit. After repentance and forgiveness, it is easy and effortless to say, with my whole being, "You are the Lord my God."

There is one more element that sticks out for me about Alma's account. He describes his soul as "harrowed up." I picture a soul that has been torn and ripped up. It is like a rototiller has churned up Alma's soul. This image gives a vivid sense of his pain, but it also tells us one more thing about experiences with God and humility. The image could mean that before this experience Alma had a soul that was like hard-packed soil. Nothing can grow in soil like that. It was not until Alma saw his guilt and the pain his actions had caused that the harrow could break up his hard-packed soul. In this newly loosened soil, the seeds of hope and faith could be planted and could grow. When the soul is hard-packed and resistant, the harrow seems awful and its pain seems dreadful. But after the harrow has done its work and when the soil can produce and sustain life, the harrow is seen as a difficult but important blessing. Alma did not choose to experience this harrow, this tilling up of his hard-packed soul, but he did respond with faith and hope to it. Perhaps this is why Alma could see the difference between being compelled to be humble versus choosing to be humble when he spoke with the Zoromites (see Alma 32:16).

I'm counting on the fact that you have felt the power of God's redeeming love when you have repented and been forgiven. I'm also guessing that experiences like this were fundamental to Greg, Jerilyn, Marty, and Brett's humility. They could submit to God because they had experienced God's love and power.

Along with Alma the Younger's dramatic repentance story, there is another Book of Mormon story that also relates a common experience. I think that this is also something Greg, Jerilyn, Marty, and Brett experienced. I'm counting on the fact that you have as well. We don't know very much about this particular story. We know even less about the people involved. Here's the story: after the destruction in the Americas after Christ's death, the survivors heard a voice. That voice told them: "ye shall offer for a sacrifice unto me a broken heart and a contrite spirit. And whoso cometh unto me with a broken heart and a contrite spirit, him will I baptize with fire and with the Holy Ghost" (3 Nephi 9:20). But then that voice gave an example of this baptism with fire: "even as the Lamanites, because of their faith in me at the time of their conversion, were baptized with fire and with the Holy Ghost, and they knew it not" (3 Nephi 9:20). That is the key element of the story—as part of their conversion, the Lamanites passed through a baptism of fire and the Holy Ghost but, somehow, they didn't realize it.

How could someone offer a broken heart and a contrite spirit and be baptized with fire and the Holy Ghost and not know it? My guess is that while your life, like mine, may have times with powerful experiences with God, and especially with experiences like forgiveness, I think that all of us pass through a life-long, slow, subtle, and imperceptible change that God brings about in us from day-to-day. This slow, steady, yet fiery change burns away our flaws while the Holy Ghost warms our hearts with love for God and others. In your daily life, as you offer a prayer here, read your scriptures there, or do seemingly small acts of kindness or service, all of these actions gradually and imperceptibly change you into someone who is more like God. The Holy Ghost's purifying influence and comforting reassurance are a slow burn. Your small changes and this slow burn baptize you, renew you, and remake you. They make God more real for you. As you become more like God, as God becomes more real to you, and as you come to know God better, it is easier and even natural for you to be submissive, committed, and devoted to God. You can trust God when you are asked to give something up (Greg), when God promises something that might seem too good to be true (Jerilyn), when God uses others to bless your life (Marty), and when God clarifies what is God's job and what is yours (Brett). This transformation might be quite different from the dramatic encounters Melville and Alma describe, but this imperceptible process is just as significant and important.

FRIENDSHIP

Dramatic repentance experiences and subtle, life-long transformations are two complementary ways you come to know God firsthand. There is another way to talk about how you know God, but to introduce this idea, I want to play a little game. Here it is: when I say a word, you fill in the blank with its opposite. Oh, and try to do this as quickly as you can. Ready?

Day: _____
Black: _____
Dark: _____
Sad: _____
Evil: _____
Excited: _____
Asleep: _____
Disengaged: _____
Nonfiction: _____
Destruction: _____
Friendship: _____

When I would play this little game in a class I taught about pride and humility, I would try to do it fast so that when I said "friendship," at least someone in class would yell, "enemyship." Of course "enemy ship" is a boat from the opposing navy. There should be an English word "enemyship" or maybe "enemiship" that means "the state of being an enemy" as the opposite of the word "friendship." But "enemiship" is not an English word.

In fact, the real English word that means being an enemy is "enmity."

Enmity is not a word we use very often. People say things like, "Those two are serious enemies" rather than saying "Those two have a lot of enmity." Because we don't use "enmity" very often, it is easy to misunderstand what C.S. Lewis and President Benson mean when they talk about pride. In President Benson's famous talk on pride, the prophet quotes from Lewis' *Mere Christianity* and says that "the central feature of pride is enmity—enmity toward God and enmity toward our fellowmen." I will return to this quote again when I talk about humility in your relationships with others, but for now I want to focus on humility in your relationship with God. If pride means seeing God as the enemy, then humility means seeing God as a friend.

Of course when you say "You are the Lord my God" with all of your heart, might, mind, and strength, you are not seeing God as your enemy. In my life, when I feel out of tune with God, when I am selfish or angry or envious or lustful, God not only seems far away, but God feels like my enemy. At those times the commandments seem like barbed wire, with me on one side and what I want on the other. In fact, I can fairly easily see how in tune I am with God by simply asking, "do I see God as an enemy right now, or do I see God as a friend?" It is amazing how much I can learn about myself by just honestly asking that question.

But to really make this idea of friendship and humility come alive for me, I picture a dark room with wooden floors and an exposed-beam ceiling. I picture a few lamps casting long shadows. And I picture the scene as rather serious. There are at least twelve men in the room, and recently one left in sort of a hurry. Most of the men are nervous but excited. They are optimistic. They are about to go from being rather poor and unimportant people to being high, powerful officials. They are even arguing about who gets what job in the new government. The new government is going to be awesome, partly because it isn't totally new. The new government will be a renewal of the great government in the past, the government ruled by King David. These eleven disciples believe that the Man they are with is the promised Messiah, the Anointed One. They believe He will kick out the Romans and establish or re-establish God's kingdom on the earth. When we read John chapter 15 now, we know that a painful reversal is just over the horizon for Jesus' followers who are with him at the Last Supper.

At this final meal, we learn something wonderful about friendship. Jesus promises His disciples that they can be connected to Him, and that through that connection they can have all of the blessings or the "fruits" God offers (John 15:1–11). Jesus commands them to love one another, and then he says these words about friendship: "You are my friends if you do what I command you" (John 15:14 NRSV). Jesus invites these followers to have a special closeness or intimacy with Him. In fact, after this He continues, "I do not call you servants any longer, because the servant does not know what the master is doing; but I have called you friends, because I have made known to you everything that I have heard from my Father (John 15:15 NRSV)." Servants merely do as they are told; friends understand, participate, and cooperate in a deeper, more intimate way.

Can you imagine being Christ's friend? Can you imagine the sort of closeness that comes with understanding better what God is doing in your life and the lives of those around you? Does this seem extraordinary? God has said something similar when the Lord told Joseph Smith, "And again I say unto you, my friends, for from henceforth I shall call you friends, it is expedient that I give unto you this commandment, that ye become even as my friends in days when I was with them, traveling to preach the gospel in my power" (D&C 84:77). This idea of being God's friends is clearly not limited to the men at the Last Supper. In fact, Christ seems to set the conditions for this friendship, this special relationship: "you are my friends if you do what I command you."

Have you ever felt this sort of closeness with God? Have you felt like you are not merely a servant on a "need-to-know" basis, but instead you are a friend, someone who enjoys the intimacy that comes with friendship? Perhaps you felt this, like I have, when you were a missionary or when you were struggling to love and support your spouse or your children. Perhaps you felt this closeness in a particularly challenging calling or trial. God may not have told you everything, but you were given more insight than what some distant boss might share with a new employee. Have you noticed that your friendship with God has been tested, strengthened, and reinforced during some of your most challenging moments? Those painful experiences that stretch you also connect you with God. In other words, often it is "only in the heart of quickest perils, only on the profound unbounded sea," that the "fully invested God can be truly and livingly found out." It is there that you come to know and experience God as a friend.

Greg, Jerilyn, Marty, and Brett are humble because they know God. They experienced God firsthand in experiences like repentance and forgiveness, and in the day-to-day, imperceptible transformation God is bringing about in them. They can say "You are the Lord My God" with their whole being, but also with a particular conviction and affection. They can say it as God's friends.

But, as you know, even as you work to be close to God, to be God's friend, the difference between you and God is obvious. In fact, the more you try to be like God, the more apparent that difference becomes. It is in those times that you might see most clearly your weakness. The place of weakness and its connection with humility is exactly what we will explore in the next chapter.

COMPLEMENTS, PARTNERS, AND FLUENT MISSIONARIES

3

PENIA, POROS, AND LOVE

In the last chapter I had you picture some men in a dark room with a wooden floor and an exposed-beam ceiling. Now I want you to picture other men in a room that is not as dark. I'm not sure if the new room has a wooden floor with an exposed-beam ceiling. It might have a marble floor. Probably not, but maybe. The men in this room are all in a very good mood. A very good mood! Maybe too good of a mood. The other men may have been drinking, but these men are drinking a lot, and some are probably at least a little drunk. Or maybe really drunk. And this isn't the Last Supper in Jerusalem. This is a dinner party in Athens. There are some famous Athenians at this party, including a political leader named Alcibiades and a playwright named Aristophanes.

They have already had dinner, and now they are lounging around, drinking, and conversing. This part of the meal is called the "symposium," which literally means to drink together. During this part of the party everyone offers an impromptu speech about a given topic. The topic for tonight is love. Everyone takes a turn, offering ideas interwoven into stories about the nature of love. One of the last speakers is Socrates. We find the story of this particular drinking discussion in Plato's *Symposium*.

When Socrates takes his turn, his central idea is that love is the drive that moves people to excellence. Love for him is not about affection or friendship. Love also doesn't have anything to do with a divine being who genuinely cares about individual mortals. Socrates' idea is that love is the motivating passion to grow, to improve, and to learn. Love is the passion that makes remarkable politicians, skillful playwrights, and great philosophers. In order to vividly describe love, Socrates recounts a discussion he had with a wise woman named Diotima. Diotima tells a story describing love's nature. The story goes like this: on the day of Aphrodite's birth, at a banquet held by the gods, one of the party's guests was the god Poros. Poros is the Greek word for Resource or Resourcefulness. He is the son of Ingenuity, so he knows how to get what he wants. Meanwhile, Penia, which is the Greek word for Poverty, arrives at the party begging for food and drink, of which there was an abundance. While Penia or Poverty is hanging around, she notices that Poros or Resource is so drunk that he has passed out in Zeus' garden. This gives Poverty the idea that if she could have a child with Resource, then this child might help her get what she always needs. Penia ends up having a child with Poros, and that child is Love.

So what does this imaginative (though not really fit for *For the Strength of Youth!*) story about Poros (Resource) and Penia (Poverty) tell us about love? Socrates explains that Love, because of his mother, is often poor, barefoot, and homeless, sleeping on the ground or on the street. The English word "penury," which means extreme poverty, is related to the name Penia. Love experiences this extreme poverty, this penury. But, since Love's father is Poros or Resourcefulness, he is always on the lookout for the best, the greatest, and the most beautiful. His resourceful nature makes him brave, determined, and crafty. With such contradictory parents, Love might be empty and searching in the morning, by afternoon his plans and schemes may have provided him with plentitude and bounty, but then, by evening, he could be hungry once again. Love's life is a constant bouncing between hunger, or seeing a need and wanting that need filled, and fulfillment, the joy that comes when his powers, abilities, and resourcefulness satisfy his needs.

Let's keep in mind that this whole story is told by a teacher and a philosopher. In fact, the story of Love as the child of Poros and Penia gives a delightful version of what we can call a love of learning. I'll give an example from my own life. A few years ago I started organizing pick-up soccer games for the faculty and staff at the university where I work. People showed up to get a little exercise, to have fun, and to get to know one another. Over the years that we have been playing, many different people have come out to kick around with us. We've expanded it to include people from the community, and some of them, particularly the young people, have tremendous skills. It is fun and inspiring to play with them. I get to see their skills, skills that I lack. I admire how they can make such accurate, powerful shots, how cleverly they pass the ball or defend, or how they can use a few moves to get out of a difficult spot. I want to be a better soccer player. I see skills that I lack. I watch them carefully to see where and how they do what they do. I will even watch some online videos that explain certain skills. And then I practice and try to train myself to do those skills at the right place and time. Seeing my lack or poverty in certain skills is the Penia portion of my Love for becoming a better soccer player. My ability to observe, practice, and work is the resourcefulness, the Poros part. In some respects, this describes all learning: you realize that you lack a knowledge of Isaiah or of blogging or of making crème brûlée or of potty training or of the subjunctive in Spanish and then you do something about it, like take a class, read a book, study on your own, find an expert to help you, or Google it.

POVERTY AND GOD'S POROS OR GRACE

There is a deeper connection that can be made with this imaginative story. This connection shows another side of humility. Humility, as described already, is the submission, commitment, and devotion evident in saying with your whole being, "You are the Lord my God." But humility also seems to be a willingness to see how you need God. Humility is about clearly seeing what you lack, where you are empty, what you need, and how you fall short. In this respect, humility, like Penia, is a beggar.

To see the connection between Penia's extreme need and humility, picture a guy writing. He is not on a computer and does not have a pen. He has an incising tool, something to make deep, lasting grooves in metal. His work is difficult and time-consuming, but the physical effort is not really what is so exhausting. In fact, there are at least three other things that make writing difficult for Moroni. The first of those three things is that Moroni has seen a vision of the people who will read his book. He knows about their struggles and challenges. He wants to give them everything they might need to come unto Christ and find happiness in this life and joy in the life to come. Moroni's second challenge is something that he has read: the writings of the Brother of Jared. Moroni finds that the Brother of Jared's writing, which includes a vision of the Savior and of everyone to walk the earth, is so powerful that the reader feels overwhelmed. Such powerful writing leads to Moroni's third concern: his writing is very inadequate. Picture Moroni, especially as we see him in the twelfth chapter of Ether. This man loves his readers (and those people are you and me), and he is trying to communicate the most important messages. Moroni knows that conveying this message can be very, very powerful, as he sees in the Brother of Jared's writing. But Moroni sees the difference and feels like he is coming up short. He sees the richness of the message, the power of the Brother of Jared's words, and then sees the lack in his own writing.

Seeing this lack, this poverty, Moroni turns to the Lord. He worries that his audience will not be persuaded because of how awkward the writing is. He worries that they will merely mock. Perhaps he wants God to make him write as powerfully as the Brother of Jared, but that is not how God responds. The Lord does not take away Moroni's weakness. God does not give him power like the power that was given to the Brother of Jared. Instead, while pointing out that foolish people mock, God gives a remarkable, powerful insight to Moroni: God's grace is sufficient for the meek.

What exactly does that phrase mean, and how might it relate to Penia and Poros? I believe that God's promise to Moroni is that God's grace gives the meek all that they need. And what is the need here? The need, the poverty here, is Moroni's lack of power in saying what he wants to say. His audience's need is the power to understand his message. His readers may lack the ability to see beyond the writing's awkwardness. Moroni sees that poverty, and he wants something to make up the difference. But God does not give Moroni that power. God's grace is that power. God's grace is the Poros, the resource, ability, or power to provide what Moroni cannot provide. God's grace gives power to meek readers so that they are touched and persuaded by Moroni's message.

This idea that God's grace is the Poros, the resource, ability, or power that overcomes the poverty, is reinforced when God instructs and reassures a struggling Moroni that God gives everyone weakness. This weakness allows us to see our poverty. When you and I see our poverty, when we then respond by faithfully and wholeheartedly saying, "You are the Lord my God," then God's power and grace give us all we need.

Though it was many years ago, I found this when my friend Greg got sick. Immediately after I learned about Greg's diagnosis, I poured out my heart to God. I felt alone and afraid. As I prayed, I felt a powerful assurance that God knew me and loved me, that God knew and loved Greg, and that God would do everything necessary to bless our lives. I do not recall God telling me Greg would recover, but I do remember the blessing of peace and assurance. I felt poor, I turned to God, and God's love and grace provided what I needed.

From what I recall, Greg was also strengthened in his weakness. His video testimony includes his moving witness of God's love and power in spite of the fact that God did not use such power to heal him. Jerilyn, when we spoke, talked about turning to the Lord when she felt confused or unsure. In her poverty she found God's resources of peace and strength. Marty found similar power and strength as God worked through other people, and Brett found that he could trust God and trust himself to make good decisions, to honor the priesthood, and to remember his covenants.

This experience of seeing a lack, a need, a poverty, and then seeing God's grace as an essential resource to address that need, an experience Greg, Jerilyn, Marty, and Brett all had, is powerful and life-changing. It is also common. The most fundamental version of this experience is repentance: the experience of seeing the impact of your sins, the poverty that those sins and weakness reduce you to, and the need for power, for redemption, for a Savior. I believe that similar experiences happen often in everyone's life, especially in a life as God's friend. We see how we could be more diligent in our church service, more patient with our children or spouse or someone at work. We see how our pettiness, our fears, our selfishness, our procrastination, our envy, how our faults and shortcomings make us poor and needy. We are like the people who respond to King Benjamin's message from the angel. We feel like we have fallen to the earth as we see our poor, needy state. In the midst of this poverty we cry out for mercy, for the application of the power and grace that comes from Christ's atoning blood. And then the Spirit of the Lord comes, fills us with joy, promises a remission of sins, and pours peace into our souls. We receive God's promised enabling power. In moments when we most desperately need a Savior, we realize that God has provided One.

One of the reasons I really like Diotima's story about Penia and Poros is that they are complements. Penia and Poros work together. Weakness has a very important role. Weakness reveals how we need God. It reveals how we need a Savior, and it makes Christ's saving power meaningful and real. We have sacred encounters with God precisely because of our weakness. Of course God wants us to overcome our weakness, and God has promised to work with us so that where we now find weakness we can someday find strength. That happens just as Diotima describes: we see our weakness, we respond to it with meekness,

God's Poros and grace provide for us, but then, over time, we see new weakness, new poverty and need, and the process continues.

HUMUS, HONESTY, VULNERABILITY, AND MEEKNESS

In the last sentence I added something: "we respond to it with meekness." Moroni was promised that God's grace is sufficient for the meek. I think we need to talk about that word, and what helps me make sense of it is something that happened a few years ago. Not long after we moved into our house, my wife and I decided that we wanted better flowerbeds in the front and in the backyard. I went to the store to buy soil, and there I learned that they have a lot of different soils. One option I could buy was humus. Humus is either nutrient-rich earth that will help support thriving plant life, or it is a clever marketing trick to get you to pay more for bags of dirt. It was while looking at those bags of dirt that I realized that there is a connection between humus, which is from the Latin word for earth or ground, and humility. When we see our weakness, we feel like King Benjamin's people felt: brought down to the ground. We feel low.

Seeing weakness brings that low, brought-down-to-the-humus, soiled feeling. But this is an important moment, because here we can choose how we will respond to this experience. This is a moment when we can reject the truth of the situation and blame someone else. Adam and Eve did exactly that. After they ate the fruit, they understood the difference between good and evil and saw their weakness. When God confronted them about it, they shifted the blame to others. This was a rookie mistake, an error made by newbies like the mistakes that little children make. Over time Adam and Eve would learn to take responsibility for their mistakes, would bravely admit to their errors, and would seek and find God's powerful grace.

The willingness to honestly acknowledge weakness requires courage. You have to be brave enough to be vulnerable. The courage to honestly and vulnerably acknowledged weakness is how I define meekness. The meek may not be particularly excited or happy about it, but they don't shy away, or slink away, or dishonestly turn away when weakness becomes evident. Meekness's courageous honesty and vulnerability then combine with humility's complete submission, commitment, and devotion in the heart-felt plea: "you are the Lord my God." When meekness and humility come together in this manner, God's power is manifest. This is the moment when God works miracles in our lives.

Penia or Poverty and Poros or Resource are opposites that complement one another in the same way that your weakness and God's matchless power and grace complement one another. Meekness and humility are partners, working together to put us in a place where God can bless and transform us.

THE NEW AND THE FLUENT MISSIONARIES

I close this section with an example that shows the roles of weakness and grace, meekness and humility, and the work of being God's friend. I call this example the new and the fluent missionaries.

The first few weeks of a mission can be rough. Besides

dealing with homesickness and the unfamiliarity of everything, a missionary might also deal with a new culture and language. Such missionaries have a hard time understanding people and speaking with them. They might feel like all they can do is smile and nod. Such new missionaries say with all of their being "You are the Lord my God" and want to be instruments God can use to bless others, but at this point they feel ineffective. You have probably seen new missionaries with a keen sense of their own inadequacy. Such missionaries see their poverty. They respond meekly, willing to courageously see how they need to improve, what they need to work on, and how God's power can bless and transform them. Perhaps you have seen how God can use these uniquely meek and humble servants. Sometimes all that these new missionaries can do is smile or nod, but they testify with their lives, with their presence, with their willingness to sacrifice, to work, and to try. In their poverty, God blesses them and everyone around them.

God uses new missionaries, but it is also good that they have experienced companions. Experienced companions can do more of the teaching and answer questions because of their skills. They are fluent missionaries. New missionaries will gradually become more fluent, and the fluency I mean is not just language skills. Missionaries learn many, many skills. They learn how to answer a wide variety of questions and concerns, how to teach much more effectively, how to speak more powerfully in church, and how to work with members, converts, companions, and mission leaders. They see where they lack, they study and pray, and they meekly and humbly strive to turn weakness into strength. Those strengths will make them more effective tools in God's hands. They know how to communicate with patience, empathy, insight, sensitivity, and skill. Skills and experience transform novices into powerful, fluent missionaries. For fluent missionaries, their skills become so natural, so second nature, that they use them effortlessly. Fluent missionaries feel God's power and love flow through them, and that love blesses everyone around them.

Fluent missionaries bring together what I have put forward about humility. Everything about their lives say to God, "You are the Lord my God," including their complete devotion and sacrifice. They willingly, honestly, and vulnerably see their weakness and seek God's enabling power. They have powerful experiences with God as well as the steady transformation or the slow burn that comes with the gift of the Holy Ghost. These missionaries may feel a close friendship with the Lord as they cooperate in this divine work.

We are all on the continuum between the novice missionary and the fluent missionary in the work God has for us. In our divinely appointed work in our homes, our callings, our jobs, or with our family and friends, sometimes we feel woefully inadequate. It feels like all we can do is smile and nod and hope that God's grace can touch others through our love and willingness. Sometimes we feel like we have some skills that God can use. And sometimes, after study, practice, and effort, we can feel more skillful and fluent in what our Heavenly Parents want us to do. It can feel wonderful to have your skills and your fluencies come together with God's love and grace to bless others.

Humility is central to this transformation. It is central to your relationship with God. In addition, humility has a role in your relationships with other people, but, of course, that humility is different from the complete submission, commitment, and devotion that you are commanded to give only to God. What humility is in your relationships with others and how you can cultivate that humility are the topics of the book's next sections.

HUMILITY IN YOUR RELATIONSHIPS WITH OTHERS

KENT, CORDELIA, AND MARTY'S FRIENDS 4

IMPORTANT NOTE

Think about the word "faith." You can have "faith" in many things. You can have "faith" that if you study, you will learn. A coach can have "faith" in her best free throw shooter. A spouse can be "faithful." But all of those uses of "faith" are quite different from faith in the Lord Jesus Christ. And just as "faith" in the Lord Jesus Christ is very different from "faith" in others or other things, so humility in your relationship with God is very different from humility in your relationships with others.

I want to put a thick black line at the top of this chapter and section of the book. I want that line there to make sure you know that there is a big difference between humility toward God and humility in your relationships with others. All of that should be obvious, but let me state it again: humility's complete submission, commitment, and devotion in saying "You are the Lord my

God" should only be said to God, and "humility" in your relationships with others is something fundamentally different. In fact, humility in your relationships with others is . . . wait . . . let me tell you a story first.

KENT

To get at what it means to be humble in your relationships with others, we are going to spend time with a man named Kent, Kent's boss, and Kent's boss's daughter. Kent is a government employee, and he has been at his job for many years. Kent's boss has recently announced his retirement, and, though Kent might be part of the transition team for the new administration, I'm guessing that once things are in place, Kent and his boss will be getting a condo in Florida. I picture Kent and his boss moving to some place calm and restful, perhaps a gulf coast active adult community where they can golf and play canasta. Of course the only problem with this plan is that Kent lives in medieval England and he happens to find himself in one of Shakespeare's tragedies, so, you know, no Florida. Oh, and this isn't going to turn out well.

Now that he is retiring, Kent's boss is turning things over to his children. He has two married daughters and a third daughter who looks to get married quite soon. He has already divided up the company, which in this case happens to be a kingdom, but before leaving he seems to want some last-minute reassurance. Kent's boss's name is Lear, and at the ceremony where he is announcing the kingdom's division, he requests impromptu speeches from his three daughters. Lear's first two daughters offer glowing, flattering, and over-the-top praise of their father. They promise unchanging, eternal love for him. The third daughter does not know what to say to her father. This daughter knows her sisters are not telling the truth about what they actually think about him. The third daughter does not want to be dishonest like her sisters. This third daughter's speech fails to flatter King Lear, and he angrily explodes.

It is at this point, the point when the title character in Shakespeare's tragedy *King Lear* flies into a rage, that his advisor and friend Kent tries to step in. Kent starts by reminding Lear that through the years Kent has served and honored the king. Lear seems to know what Kent might say, so he says this: "the bow is bent and drawn. Make from the shaft." Lear is telling Kent that his authority and anger are about to execute his judgment like an arrow flying from a bow. Lear doesn't want Kent to be caught in the crossfire. In spite of this furious threat, Kent doesn't turn away. Kent tells the king, "let it fall rather, though the fork invade the region of my heart." Kent requests that the king let the arrow fall to the ground instead of being shot, or, if the arrow must be shot, Kent is willing to let it hit him. Kent explains that it would be "unmannerly" or inappropriate for him to not step in when the king is clearly making a mistake. He tells the king that it is his duty to speak when deceitful flattery is causing the king to fall into folly. Kent advises the king to not give up the kingdom just yet and to not act rashly. To prove the value of his advice, Kent tells the king to use Kent's life and character as the measurement of the wisdom of his recommendations.

In spite of Kent's wise counsel, Lear responds "Kent, on thy life, no more." Lear wants Kent to be quiet, but Kent replies "my life I never held but as a pawn to wage against thine enemies." Kent says he has been like a pawn in a chess match. He has willingly allowed the king to use him. As he has always served the king, he refuses to back down now in spite of the king's threats. Lear angrily shouts, "out of my sight!" to which Kent responds, "see better." Kent's actions, character, words, and whole being are focused on helping the king see what is really going on. Kent wants Lear to see better.

As the argument continues, Lear accuses Kent of trying to "make us break our vows." Lear goes so far as to accuse Kent of pride, and finally orders that he be banished from the kingdom. But Kent's commitment to the king is such that he doesn't actually leave. Instead he puts on a disguise and figures out a way to become the king's servant yet again. He accompanies the king in this disguise and does what he can to help and protect him. But even the Fool can see that working for a king who no longer has power will get you into trouble. And trouble soon finds Kent. Kent ends up in the stocks when his appeal to the king's authority cannot protect him. Once Lear's older two daughters and their husbands have all of the power, they mistreat the king so badly that he has a mental breakdown. Over time, the king's power and mental faculties continue to decline, but still Kent attends to him and helps him as best he can. Kent eventually takes Lear to the safety of an invading French army, but, spoiler alert, Kent cannot prevent Lear's own death from a broken heart at the end of the play.

CORDELIA

Kent's response to Lear is key to understanding humility, but before I explain the connection between Kent and humility, I need to talk about Cordelia. Cordelia is Lear's third and youngest daughter. Lear plans on giving her the largest portion of the kingdom, but her speech so displeases him that he disowns her. Where Cordelia's sisters heap heavy praise on the king and proclaim their complete devotion, Cordelia tells the king, "I love your Majesty according to my bond, no more nor less." This is not enough for Lear. She tries to explain that she appropriately obeys, loves, and honors her father, but her defense only makes him angrier. As he did with Kent, Lear accuses Cordelia of pride. After Lear divides the land he planned on giving to Cordelia between her older sisters, the man who was going to marry Cordelia goes back on his vow. Another suiter, who happens to be the King of France, believes that Cordelia is still a valuable, worthy wife and willingly marries her.

As the play continues and Lear descends further and further into mental instability, Cordelia does what she can to help and rescue her father. Over the course of the tragedy, Lear is reduced from a king with royal robes to a naked man sleeping in a mud hut. When Cordelia eventually finds her broken father, she has him cleaned up, clothed, medically treated, and delivered to her. In her presence, Lear begins to come to. He mistakes Cordelia for an angel that has visited his tormented soul in hell. As he is still unsure of his condition and location, Cordelia kneels before him and pleads, "Oh, look upon me, sir." The one who has rescued him, Cordelia, asks for Lear to look at her. This could simply be to help restore his bearings, but in another sense Cordelia wants Lear to really see her. We recall that Lear did not really see her before. When Lear looks at her now, he cannot believe what he sees. He is afraid he is being tormented or mocked. A disbelieving Lear says, "I think this lady to be my child Cordelia." The weeping Cordelia responds simply and affirmatively, "And so I am, I am." Lear's first words to her are "Be your tears wet?" Lear does not seem to believe that she is really crying for him. Overwhelmed and in disbelief, Lear asks her not to weep. He tells her, "If you have poison for me I will drink it." Lear now recognizes her, and he recalls how he mistreated her. He continues, "I know you do not love me, for your sisters have, as I do remember, done me wrong. You have some cause; they do not." Lear recognizes his mistakes and is even willing to take what he might judge as a proper punishment. Lear believes that Cordelia could not love him. Lear probably believes this because Cordelia's sisters flatteringly claimed to love him but turned out to have been lying. Lear believed them, and now he seems to think that everyone is like them. He could be thinking that if those he believed and those he entrusted with everything did not really love him, how could the one he did not believe, the one he disinherited, and the one he banished possibly love him? At this moment Cordelia could mention all of the hardships she has passed through since being disowned. She could provide a long, angry list of slights, insults, and injuries. She seems to have many, many reasons.

Instead, Cordelia looks intently and lovingly at her father and says, "No cause, no cause." Cordelia does not hold accusations, claims, grudges, offenses, or causes against her father. Now that he has returned to her and to his senses, Cordelia is glad to be with him again.

HUMILITY, COMMITMENT, AND MARTY'S FRIENDS

Cordelia and Kent are lovingly committed to Lear in spite of his terrible mistakes. That wise and loving commitment is humility. Of course they do not submit to Lear as if he were God in spite of the fact that Lear seems to believe that they should. No one should ever submit, commit, or be dedicated to another person like that. In addition, Cordelia and Kent are Lear's true friends. When Lear berates them, accuses them of pride, banishes them, dishonors, and disowns them, they choose to not see Lear as their enemy. Resisting enmity and embracing friendship is another aspect of their humility.

Cordelia and Kent show two sides of friendship, and, by extension, humility. One side of friendship is that friends call you out when you are foolish. Friends don't just go along with whatever you might say, do, or plan. Kent bravely opposes Lear when he foolishly believes the empty flattery of his older daughters. Kent stands up and says something when Lear does not see Cordelia's truth and sincerity. Kent will not back down when Lear fails to see accurately what is really going on. When you are mistaken, friends tell you to "see better." Friends also look for ways to help you see the truth. Sometimes friends disguise themselves, metaphorically, to help you out and to lead you to the best outcome. Friends, in humility, are wisely and lovingly committed to you and your growth.

Friends also value you above other considerations. It is the friendly, loving, devoted face of Cordelia that brings Lear back from his breakdown. At first, Lear doesn't seem to be able to focus. He then has a hard time believing what he sees. When Lear finally does see her, he doesn't see her clearly. He still seems to see Cordelia's sisters, those who had lied to him and mistreated him. He also seems to see and recall how poorly he treated Cordelia. Cordelia, in contrast, doesn't see any of that. Cordelia sees Lear. Cordelia sees a way to help her father, and she sees a way to be reconnected with him. At the very moment when Cordelia could have seen the many ways that Lear caused her pain, instead of seeing any possible "causes," Cordelia's humble commitment to her father allows her to see him and to love him. Humility's friendship is helping friends see and embrace the truth. Humility's friendship encourages others so that they can bravely grow and move beyond foolish mistakes and weakness.

As I was working on this first chapter in the section about humility in relationships with others, it reminded me of my conversation with Marty, the man who participated in the church's Addiction Recovery Program. I called up Marty and told him what I had so far for the chapter, and he said that friendship, truth telling, encouraging the growth of others, and valuing others in spite of weakness and foolishness are things he found in attending ARP meetings. He told me that the first meetings he went to were terrifying. He lives in an area with a lot of members of the church, and he was afraid of who might see him there. He didn't know what to expect, and he had never admitted to others that he felt powerless in the face of his weakness. He said that in the first meeting he hardly said anything, but that over time he became comfortable saying more and more. Eventually those meetings felt like a safe haven. ARP meetings became a place where he could allow others to see what he was most ashamed of. Marty said that he could not believe the outpouring of love he felt when he was brave enough to open up. He also mentioned that, besides feeling incredible joy from the compassion that others extended to him, Marty found it wonderful to extend compassion to others. The compassion he felt and extended seemed to drain away the poisonous shame and fear. It was also great to see that the compassion he extended could clear away similar toxins for others. Finally, Marty said that simple text messages where people asked for help or shared notes of encouragement made a huge difference in finding strength where there had once been weakness.

Marty's experience points out one more thing about humility. I started the chapter by saying that humility to God, which is complete submission, commitment, and devotion, is as different from humility in our relationships with others as faith in the Lord Jesus Christ is different from faith in others. Marty's experience shows that commitment to others leads them to God. The friends that Marty found in ARP did exactly that. Marty's friends extended compassion that removed shame and fear. That compassion encouraged strength where there had been weakness. Marty's friends worked with God to do God's work in Marty's life. Those friends provided assistance Marty could not get alone.

Growth and salvation seem to require a group effort. We form bonds with one another, we knit our hearts together, we mourn with each other, comfort each other, and lift each other because we cannot make it alone. God uses each of us to assist and to bring about the growth of others. In order to do God's work, we have to be humble. We have to be completely submissive, committed, and devoted to God. We also have to be lovingly and wisely committed to others. That can mean wisely, carefully calling others out when they are foolish like what Kent did. It can mean lovingly looking beyond the pain others have caused in the past to encourage their growth in the present like what Cordelia did. It means extending compassion to everyone and encouraging others so that God can help others find strength where there was once weakness.

Cordelia and Kent show slightly different commitments because each has a different relationship with Lear. Cordelia, as Lear's daughter, cannot confront him in quite the same way that Kent can. That distinction actually turns out to be quite important, since, as we will see, humility toward other people means something slightly different depending upon the relationship. The next chapters will explore how humility in relationships of equals, like between spouses or siblings, is different from the humility we find in unequal relationships, like relationships between parents and children, teachers and students, coaches and members of the team, employers and employees, therapists and clients, and leaders and followers.

HUMILITY IN RELATIONSHIPS WITH EQUALS, OR WHY JANE CAN'T FIND THE MEDIUM 5

JANE

Jane is writing this story about ten years after it happened. She is now in her early thirties, married, and has a child. Hindsight lets her see things clearer. She has become a much more independent woman, but that independence did not come all at once. She's thinking back on one particular day with her cousin, a man ten years her senior. This cousin was a very devout, religious man. Even his given name is St. John. He was the parson of the local church, a man willing to venture out no matter what the time of day or what the weather was in order to minister to the needs of his local congregation. She respects and admires him. But something about him bothers her.

She is remembering a day when she had just received a letter. Jane had thought it would be from someone she misses and is quite worried about, but it was only some legal or financial business. She sits down to study with St. John. She is having a hard time concentrating and starts to cry. Her cousin allows her time to compose herself and then tells her that they will take a walk. She suggests that her other cousins, St. John's sisters, join them. He tells her that she must be his only companion. He tells her what to wear, to go out through the kitchen, and take a particular road.

Looking back on this moment, Jane concludes that she never knew a "medium." She writes, "I never in my life have known any medium in my dealings with positive, hard characters." What she means by "hard characters" is dominating people. She means people who have a will that is "antagonistic to her own." When she says "medium," she means that she cannot find a middle between what she calls "absolute submission" and, on the opposite end, "determined revolt." It troubled Jane that she cannot find that middle. She reflects that she would "always faithfully observed the one," in this case the first one, absolute submission, "up to the very moment of bursting, sometimes with volcanic vehemence, into the other." That "other" is determined revolt. As she looks back, she sees how, when working with strong-willed people, she would try to find a middle and would start by going along with whatever that strong-willed person wanted, but then she would eventually blow up and go in the opposite direction.

Jane tells another story about agreeing and going along and then later going in the opposite direction. It is a story about absolute submission bursting like a volcano into determined revolt. When Jane was ten, she was living with her aunt and cousins. These were different cousins from St. John and his sisters. Her aunt was cruel and insensitive. Once, another cousin, a mean and domineering bully, assaulted her. She tried to stop his attack. By the time the aunt found the children, she punished Jane. Normally Jane, a little girl at the time, would be quiet and docile when her aunt punished her. On this occasion she exploded. She describes her volcano-like response to her aunt as a mutiny. Jane even calls herself a "rebel slave."

So why can't Jane find a middle? Why can't Jane find a medium between absolute submission and determined revolt? Why can't she just be humble, or at least learn to properly balance humility and self-assertion?

To explain why Jane cannot find a middle, we can look at one more story from her life. When she was about eighteen, Jane left the school where she had grown up. She had recently been working there. She left to take a job as a governess. While working as a governess, she fell in love with the child's guardian/her employer. She, of course, did not mean to fall in love with him, and was especially disturbed that, by all appearances, this man, Edward Fairfax Rochester, was going to marry a beautiful, wealthy, and talented woman of his same social class. Because of that expectation, Jane does not understand him when Rochester indirectly asks Jane to marry him. Not understanding that he's proposing to her, she tells him she will be leaving. When he tells her he wants her to stay, she still does not realize it is to be his wife. She becomes upset with him, saying that staying while he's marrying someone else would be too painful for her. She goes so far as to speak to her employer and the master of the house in ways that go against the expected social norms of her time. Jane justifies breaking those norms because it is "her spirit speaking." She says it this way: "it is my spirit that addresses your spirit; just as if both had passed through the grave, and we stood at God's feet, equal,—as we are!" In Jane's eyes, her and Rochester are, in spirit, equals. Moments later, during the same conversation, Rochester, trying to clear up the confusion about who he wants to marry, says to Jane, "My bride is here because my equal is here, and my likeness." He then clearly and simply asks her to marry him.

Jane Eyre believes that she and Rochester are equals. He calls her his equal and offers to marry her as his equal. A central point of this chapter is that equality is the fundamental reason why Jane cannot find a middle. Jane cannot find a medium between "absolute submission and determined revolt" when she is not treated as an equal.

THE LANGUAGE OF REQUEST AND RESPECT

Dr. John Lund explains why the lack of proper treatment as an equal is the reason that Jane cannot find a middle in her relationship with her cousin St. John. In his book *For All Eternity*, Lund describes different relationship categories. One category is relationships of equals. Relationships of equals include those between friends, siblings, fellow students, fellow team members, coworkers, ward or branch members, and spouses. For Lund, there is language appropriate for relationships of equals. He calls this the language of "request and respect." Here are some examples of that language: I may say to a friend, "I have a favor to ask, but I understand if you cannot do it." A spouse might ask, "do you want my opinion about that decision?" You might say to a sibling or a coworker, "are you sure that is a good idea?" Someone at a ward council might say "how about if we do this instead?" I might say to a fellow student or to my father-in-law, "I'm not sure I see it that way."

For Lund, the language of request and respect, the language used with equals, is, of course, respectful. This language makes requests instead of demands. It honors the other as an equal. This language never tells another person what they ought to do, should do, or need to do. The opposite of the language of request and respect is what Lund calls "directive language." Lund explains that directive language is proper for parents, teachers, coaches, bosses, therapists, and other leaders. It is language suited to those who direct. In such unequal relationships like parents and children or bosses and employees, it is appropriate for one to tell the other "I need you to," "I want you to," "you ought to" and "you should." It is perfectly appropriate for a boss to tell an employee, "you need to arrive on time" or "I want that report by 4:45." It is appropriate for a coach to tell her players, "you need to pick up the pace" or "you should practice at least 100 free throws each week." It is also appropriate for a parent to tell a child, "you ought to keep better track of the time" and "you should write down when your assignments are due and then do them in advance" and "you need to wear deodorant, no, really, you really need to wear deodorant!"

To see the difference between the language of request and respect and directive language, think about some alternatives. Imagine if a sibling told you, "well, what you should really do is finally get your act together." Imagine if a coworker said, "of course you ought to have worked harder so you can make sure to get that report in by 4:45." Imagine if a spouse said, "you need to either work harder and earn more money or you need to spend less on stuff for yourself."

How did you feel as you read those sentences? Did you feel annoyed, as if someone were poking you in the shoulder? Did you feel a tightening inside? Did you feel a little claustrophobic, like the walls were slowly moving in around you? Did these sentences sound like nagging? Annoyance, tightening, claustrophobia, and nagging--these are some of the negative experiences that come when you use directive language with equals.

But, you might ask, isn't it appropriate from time to time for a spouse or sibling to tell the other spouse or another sibling what he or she ought, should, or needs to do? Is it really so bad to use directive language in relationships with equals? When Lund describes why directive language is not appropriate for relationships with equals, he points out that when people in equal relationships use directive language, they are attempting to boss or to parent the other person. When someone tells an equal, "you ought" or "you should" or "you need to do this or that," that person not only acts like a parent, but they put the other person in an impossible situation. The equal is treated as the child. That "child" has two unacceptable options: follow the directive and be reduced to being a child or act against the demand and become someone who seems proud, willful, selfish, or rebellious.

To see what a problem this is, think about relationships where people should be equals, but they do not use the language of request and respect. Imagine a marriage where one spouse regularly uses directive language. That bossy spouse ends up feeling exhausted from being married to a selfish or a rebellious child. The other spouse will also feel very unsatisfied, married to someone who is nagging and condescending. One spouse who is told what that person should, ought, or needs to do by an equal inevitably feels belittled and disrespected. These spouses fall into seemingly unchangeable roles, roles that are frustrating, exhausting, and demeaning.

If you are fortunate enough that you cannot even imagine an inappropriate relationship of equals like this, we can go back to Charlotte Brontë's novel for an example. When Jane is compelled by her cousin to go on a walk with him, as described previously, he wants to talk to her alone because he has something he wants her to do. He wants her to travel abroad and work as a missionary with him. The missionary work he has in mind for Jane is not something she is well suited to do. Physically, she is rather frail. She believes she would not live very long as a missionary under such hardships. In addition, unlike St. John, she does not feel that God has called her to do that work. But St. John, anticipating her reservations, is ready to answer all of her arguments. She seems almost persuaded by him, but what she cannot agree to is that they get married. St. John sees marriage as essential. Jane, in contrast, claims that they could go abroad as missionary partners without being married. When St. John rebuffs this, Jane rejects his demand. While she is willing to trust and believe him, working with him as a missionary, she refuses to surrender herself entirely to him and be his wife.

HUMILITY AMONG EQUALS

Reading this conflict in *Jane Eyre* shows vividly that St. John does not see Jane as an equal. Perhaps it is his age or his powerful religious convictions, but he clearly believes he knows exactly what she ought, should, and needs to do. He puts her in an impossible position—absolute submission to him as if she were his child or determined revolt against his authority and demands. Jane cannot find a medium because no medium exists. She tries to insist that St. John see her as his equal. She wants to maintain some independence by accompanying him without marrying him. But St. John refuses even this small amount of independence. There can be no "medium" for Jane because St. John refuses to respectfully see her as his equal.

Jane's experience shows the dangers of equals using directive language. It also shows the dangers of equals refusing to respectfully acknowledge others as equals. This brings us to a central idea of this chapter: humility among equals is treating the other as a respected equal. In true humility, equals use the language of respect and request instead of directive language. To see this better, think how free and empowered Jane could have been had St. John said, "Jane, I have a request for you, but, of course, you can say no. I'd like you to accompany me as a missionary and as my wife." Jane could have freely considered the request. She could have countered that she would accompany him but not as his wife. He could have reconsidered. Even if he disagreed and if she finally turned down his request, she could have done so without the impossible alternatives of submission or revolt. Jane and St. John could have maintained and even strengthened their relationship as equals.

Humility that is appropriate for equals is, of course, very, very different from humble submission, commitment, and devotion to God. It is also different from how a child is humble toward a parent, a student toward a teacher, or an employee toward a boss. Humility in unequal relationships like those is examined in the next chapter. Humility among equals is a respectful partnership. Of course, there are times when you disagree with an equal. You may strongly disagree. You may believe that an equal is being foolish. You might do all you can to persuade them to think or to act differently. Conflicts like these may be unpleasant, but they are often part of meaningful relationships among equals. Such conflicts push equals to examine, to re-examine, to struggle, to listen, and to grow.

WHAT IF JANE HAD MARRIED ST. JOHN?

I want to touch on a dark, painful misunderstanding about humility among equals. This misunderstanding comes when equals do not treat each other as equals. Let me explain. Let's imagine that Jane had married St. John. Perhaps she would have married him because she trusted him. He tirelessly served the people in his parsonage. He has immense charity and demonstrates remarkable devotion to God. He seems trustworthy. I can imagine many people around Jane telling her to humbly trust him. People may even tell Jane that she should submit to him. She said that it seemed wrong for her to marry him, and she duly resisted, but what if she had given in and married him?

After Jane and St. John would have married, what would she do in the future when she disagreed with him? Let's imagine, for example, that Jane wanted to visit Rochester before she and St. John left for their missionary service. Or what if Jane believed strongly that they should have children before leaving? St. John might very well disagree with her on those and many, many other topics. What if she really feels that those things are important to her? What if St. John does not seem to listen to her views or feelings about those decisions? What if they get into heated discussions over those issues? If Jane and St. John were truly equals, they could disagree. They could even strongly disagree. They would have to do the difficult work of coming to the best decision for both of them. But if Jane and St. John are not respectful equals, this difficult work would be impossible. And here is why—St. John would believe that he is right and that his views should be respected and obeyed. When Jane disagrees with St. John, he will insist that she trust him. He will insist that she see things his way and recognize that he is correct. He may even insist that the role of a wife is to be humble toward the man who presides. When she feels claustrophobic or belittled or disrespected, when she feels like she is not being heard, and when she has painful and conflicted feelings, she might misunderstand those feelings as pride or as being from the devil. If she were a member of the church, she may worry that those negative feelings mean that she has "lost the Spirit." As she disagrees with him, he may assert that she is causing contention. He might tell her that the contention she is causing is not from God. She might end up feeling guilty about her very valid and even useful feelings. She might erroneously conclude that stifling those feelings is part of righteously "longsuffering." And, as the worst possible step, she might conclude that she just needs to serve more or be more charitable, kinder, or more humble.

Submitting to an equal, whether that equal is a husband, wife, or any other equal, is not humility. Submitting to an equal destroys the respect and strong friendship that should exist. Submitting to an equal robs people of the strength, esteem, and dignity that every child of our Heavenly Parents inherits from those Parents. Submitting to an equal creates an unhealthy relationship for both partners. Equals who demand, invite, or even allow submission on the part of an equal abuse the respectful, friendly, mutually affirming and mutually strengthening relationship that should exist.

Before I leave this hypothetical situation, I want to mention Greg again. Greg was my friend who died from bone cancer. I mentioned him in the first chapter. I bring up Greg for this reason—Greg had to have great faith when God asked him to give things up. Greg had to trust the Lord when he gave up his dream of getting better by Christmas or of going on a mission. Greg trusted the Lord when he had to give up his hope of surviving the cancer.

So what does Greg trusting in the Lord have to do with Jane if she had submitted to St. John? Jane, if she found herself in the situation of an unhealthy relationship of equals, would have to trust the Lord. Trusting the Lord might be very difficult. She would have to reject the idea that she just needs to serve more or be more charitable and more humble for things to work out with St. John. She would have to trust God when she learned that stifling her painful yet valid feelings is not righteous longsuffering. She would have to trust the Lord that sometimes "contention," or disagreeing with someone, even in a heated manner, can be what is best for both of them. She would have to trust the Lord that her feelings of claustrophobia, of being belittled and disrespected in her current relationship with her husband, were valid and valuable feelings. She would have to trust that those feelings told her the truth. She would have to trust the Lord as she learned to trust herself. She would have to trust the Lord as she learned how to be a respectful and duly respected equal partner in her relationship. She would have to give up her poorly placed hope that by trusting or submitting to St. John, she would get what both of them want. She might rightly be afraid that she is putting her relationship at risk. But she would have to trust the Lord that, with the God's help, she could either create a new relationship based on mutual respect or that the Lord would help her see her way forward in her life with or without St. John. Jane's complete trust in the Lord to do all of this would require tremendous faith, submission, commitment, and devotion toward God. It would truly require her to say, with all of her being, "You (and no one else) are the Lord my God."

A WONDERFUL FACT

To finish this chapter, and while I am drawing examples from British literature to make some points, I have one more example and one more point. This example is a line found toward the beginning of Charles Dickens' novel *A Tale of Two Cities*. The line is this: "A WONDERFUL fact to reflect upon, that every human creature is constituted to be that profound secret and mystery to every other." This line reminds me that I can never know what it is like in the feelings, thoughts, desires, fears, hopes, and longings of others. Other people are never completely clear or open to me. When I keep in the front of my mind the idea that others are a profound secret and a mystery to me, it is easier to have a sense of awe and wonder.

Keeping in mind that others are a secret and mystery to me has a few more advantages. This idea frees me from the need to completely figure out the people around me. I can give up the need to know them entirely and exactly. Since others are a secret and mystery to me, I'm also reminded that I can never actually judge others accurately. I cannot weigh or evaluate their feelings, thoughts, desires, fears, hopes, and longings, since I can never know all of them. This understanding not only frees me from the demands of judging others, but it reminds me that God is the only Being qualified to judge. Finally, the last advantage that the idea that others are a profound secret and mystery to me offers is that I can see that, since I cannot properly judge, what I can do is extend compassion. I can mourn with those who mourn and comfort those who need comfort. I can joy with them in their best times and suffer with them in their worst. I can be a good friend to others, avoiding directive language and instead using the language of request and respect. In my life, I rarely need other people's judgment. I do, however, cherish their genuine compassion.

One last point and I promise the chapter will be over: the value of compassion toward one another is something that brings us back to what Marty found in the Addiction Recovery Program. In that program, participants spoke about the most painful and broken sides of themselves. Yet what they found among those equals was not judgment but compassion. They did not tell each other what they should, ought, or need to do. They mourned with one another, comforted one another, and encouraged one another. No wonder that those respectful equals could be God's instruments in blessing each other's lives.

The people Marty encountered in ARP meetings helped him overcome weakness and nurtured Marty's humble submission, commitment, and devotion to God. Encouraging others, helping others overcome weakness, and nurturing their humility is what leaders do. Those efforts and a leader's humility are described in the next chapter.

HUMILITY 6
IN UNEQUAL
RELATIONSHIPS

PLANNED OBSOLESCENCE

The meeting took place on a dark and stormy night, and, all around, one could hear the echo of many clocks. Okay, I don't know if it was dark or stormy, and the only reason I assume the stuff about the clocks is because the meeting was in Switzerland. But the meeting was dark, very dark. And that is odd because it was a meeting of lightbulb makers. What was so "dark" about the lightbulb makers' Swiss meeting was this: they were plotting to make lightbulbs that would not last as long so that they could sell more lightbulbs. The group of lightbulb manufacturers was called the Phoebus Cartel. At this meeting in the 1920s, the group set a target of making bulbs that would only last about 1,000 hours. Up to this point, lightbulbs could last many thousands of hours. Not only did the Phoebus Cartel reach this target, but even today most lightbulbs last between 1,000 and 2,000 hours, in spite of the fact that lightbulb manufacturers have the know-how, or at least had the knowhow, to make bulbs that could last much, much longer.

There is a phrase for making something that you know will stop working after a certain period of time. That phrase is "planned obsolescence." It is a pretty sneaky trick that companies use to get you to buy electronic gadgets like the latest phone. Computer printers and ink cartridges makers use planned obsolescence. Publishers make textbooks in such a way that you have to buy newer versions. Computer makers and software companies make products that force you to buy updated software and then the latest computer to run that software. Cars and televisions are often made to be easier to replace with a newer one than to be repaired. Even pantyhose and nylons were once stronger and were made weaker so people would need to buy more. These are all products that could be made to be more durable, more reliable, longer-lasting, or at least easily and inexpensively updated, but instead makers plan for them to fail or at least to be obsolete.

BENEVOLENT NEGLECT WITH OCCASIONAL, WELL-TIMED INTERVENTIONS, AND ELEVATORS

Planned obsolescence is a very important element of a leader's humility, but I'm not going to explain that right now. Instead, let me tell you about my friend Mike Sanford. Mike has been teaching ceramics for many, many years at the small, liberal arts university where I work. At the time I'm writing this, Mike is about to retire, and those of us in the Art department, including the faculty, staff, and students, will miss him.

A few years ago, I was working on an article about teaching art, so I interviewed Mike. Mike has a reputation as one of the best teachers in the department and in the university. That is saying a lot, since the school is a small, private college where good teaching is the highest priority. When I want Mike to really light up during our conversations, I bring up some of the students he has worked with. He will talk about how each one developed, overcame struggles, and eventually made work that the student could be proud of. Mike will tell me what the student is doing now, which sometimes has to do with making art, but which is usually about how that former student has grown and blossomed as a person.

At one point during our conversation, Mike used a phrase that I ended up thinking about for a long time. Mike describes his approach to teaching ceramics like this: benevolent neglect with occasional, well-timed interventions. Here's what Mike seems to mean by that: Mike will explain a new process to the class. He will write and illustrate the process on the blackboard in the ceramics studio. He will demonstrate it. Then he will give the rest of the time to students to practice that new process. Some, of course, get it right off. Some will require more coaching, more assistance, and more encouragement. As the time goes by,

Mike is aware of all of the students in the class. He knows each one's skills, tendencies, and challenges. In addition, he knows that learning a new skill requires time, practice, and patience. It requires sitting with something difficult and tolerating failure and frustration. Mike lets students work, practice, and struggle. He leaves them alone, but his leaving them alone, his neglect, is to give them space to learn, struggle, and grow. Mike's neglect is not because of apathy; it is because of genuine concern and a desire to see students grow. Mike lovingly leaves them alone. But Mike, knowing his students, also realizes that there are moments when a well-timed intervention can make a big difference. Mike may see that a student does not understand a crucial element. He might notice that a student is repeating a mistake without recognizing it. He may understand that a student needs a bit of a boost, some encouragement, a smile and a pat on the back to continue to move forward. While the occasional, well-timed intervention might seem important, the time when the student is left alone is just as essential. As a great art teacher, Mike knows the value of patient, benevolent neglect as well as the occasional, well-timed intervention.

There is one more lesson that I think is useful that I learned from Mike. Many years ago, we were mentoring a student who was doing his senior work. It was good work, but I could see some ways that he could improve it. Mike agreed with what I saw. I spoke with the student, and then ended up speaking with him several more times. Each time I spoke with him, he seemed to understand what I was proposing, but it never seemed to make it into his work. I got frustrated with the student. One day I was talking with Mike about how I believed the student was not doing what we had discussed. Mike looked at me with a wry smile and said, "Shawn, I just don't think that the elevator is going to that floor." What Mike meant, of course, was that the student was not in a place artistically to use what I was suggesting. His developmental elevator was just not going to go to that floor. I recall this experience and this phrase whenever I encounter students who are just not quite at the place necessary to master a certain skill or wrap their brains around some idea. For whatever reason, their elevator is just not going to that floor right now.

PLAYING GOD

Perhaps as you read about Mike's approach to teaching ceramics you thought about some of your own experiences with God. It seems to me that God's approach to working with me is often benevolent neglect with occasional, well-timed interventions. God seems to leave me to work and struggle. Sometimes God intervenes with inspiration or encouragement. Sometimes God seems to use others to do those interventions. Sometimes I can almost feel God's smile when I'm still not quite getting something. I may be having trouble overcoming a habit or sin, or perhaps it is difficult for me to forgive someone or to take a particular risk or face some specific fear. For whatever reason, I just can't seem to do it or I just can't quite seem to stop doing it. In those moments, it sometimes feels like God's patient smile says, "well, the elevator just isn't going to that floor for you right now."

So what do you think of the idea that what Mike does as a teacher is like what God does? I call this section "playing God" because leadership, including parenting, teaching, coaching, and acting as a boss or therapist is playing God. I draw this idea of playing God from M. Scott Peck's book *The Road Less Travelled*. Peck's book explores the value of discipline, love, and spiritual growth. Peck talks about people using power to influence the spiritual growth of others. He says that this power comes with tremendous risks. Peck starts with questions you might ask yourself about why you can have power in other people's lives. He says: "Who am I to influence the course of human events? By what authority am I entitled to decide what is best for my child, spouse, my country or the human race? Who gives me the right to dare to believe in my own understanding and then to presume to exert my will upon the world?" From these initial questions, Peck reaches this final question: "Who am I to play God?"

From these questions, Peck makes these observations: "*That is the risk. For whenever we exercise power we are attempting to influence the course of the world, of humanity, and we are thereby playing God.*" Peck then combines leadership and power with love when he says, "But those who truly love, and therefore work for the wisdom that love requires, know that to act is to play God." For Peck, to be a leader of any kind, including a parent, teacher, coach, boss, therapist, or other leader, is to play God. Peck continues that, "yet (such leaders) also know that there is no alternative except inaction and impotence. Love compels us to play God with full consciousness of the enormity of the fact that

that is just what we are doing." In Peck's way of thinking, leadership in any form means playing God. Love and honesty require that you understand the importance and the heaviness of what you do. Peck even says this: "With this consciousness the loving person assumes the responsibility of attempting to be God and not to carelessly play God, to fulfill God's will without mistake. We arrive, then, at yet another paradox: only out of the humility of love can humans dare to be God." What exactly is the "humility of love" and how is it connected with leadership and playing God?

BACK TO PENIA AND POROS AND THE FLUENT MISSIONARY

To understand the "humility of love" and playing God, let's bring back Penia and Poros. Penia, as you recall, means poverty. It means seeing what you lack, what you need, and where you come up short. Loving leaders courageously see the importance of what they do. They are playing God. But those leaders see their lack. Those leaders are meek because they courageously and vulnerably see their shortcomings. Humble, loving leaders are well aware of how we can never really be equipped or prepared to fulfill God's will without mistake. They are well aware that the people that they are trying to influence are a mystery to them. But those same humble leaders know that they have to act. Not acting, not doing anything, means inaction and impotence. Such leaders bravely act in the shadow of their own inadequacy.

I think that this is exactly where God wants every leader. God wants every parent, teacher, coach, boss, therapist, and leader stuck between Penia, which is their poverty and inadequacy, and Poros, which is God's divine power and grace. God's power seems to come to life when humble leaders see their poverty or lack and when they reach out for God's resources and abundance.

To illustrate this last point, I want to go back to my friend Mike Sanford. During Mike's career, he has always worked very hard to improve as a teacher. He loves to have conversations with other instructors about what they are doing. He loves to learn from others. He very willingly takes challenges he has and seeks advice from others. He sees where he lacks, where he can improve, and he does all in his power to draw on resources to get the skills and knowledge he needs. He has practiced for many, many years, teaching thousands of students. He has learned from his experience and become more skillful. He has a better sense of when to leave a student alone and exercise some benevolent neglect and when to intervene. He knows when to push and encourage as well as when to patiently see that for now the elevator just isn't going to that floor. Time, practice, and experience have transformed him into something like the fluent missionary. Mike is someone with knowledge and skills that can encourage the growth of his students. And there is one more thing about Mike. Though he is not of our faith, his sights for his students are beyond growth as artists. Mike wants his students to grow as people. He wants them to become the best they can be, to achieve their highest potential. God uses Mike to encourage the growth of God's children. That growth draws Mike's students closer to God, even if they don't see it or are aware of it.

JUSTIN

One example of a student like this is Justin. A few years after I started working with Mike, he had a particularly promising student. Mike worked with him just like any student, but Justin really took to ceramics. Justin was so dedicated and talented that after graduating he moved to Chicago and continued his studies in a very good program. Justin continued to grow and develop as an artist as well as a teacher. Some years later, Mike had a sabbatical. This meant that instead of teaching, Mike would be able to spend his time working exclusively on his own ceramic art. The department looked for someone to temporarily teach Mike's classes, and Justin was hired. Mike worked with Justin to make his adjustment as smooth as possible, but then Mike gave him space to teach his classes as he'd like.

Mike's work with Justin helped him develop as an artist. That work prepared Justin to be successful when he went to graduate school. Those experiences made it so Justin could replace Mike when he went on sabbatical. Oddly enough, Mike's excellent teaching and leadership made him replaceable or even obsolete. Mike trained someone so well that that person could eventually replace him.

Justin brings us back to lightbulbs, electronic gadgets, printers, ink cartridges, textbooks, cars, televisions, and planned obsolescence. These objects are made to be obsolete. The people who make these products do it to force you to buy more and to be more dependent upon them. Leaders, including parents, teachers, coaches, bosses, and therapists, also embrace planned obsolescence, though in a very different way. Great leaders try to make themselves obsolete. Parents work so that their children become healthy, well-adjusted, independent adults. Teachers want students to master the material, and they want students to become independent learners. They want students to learn how to learn on their own. Coaches want players who not only have knowledge and skills, but who know how to acquire the knowledge and skills that they lack. Employers want employees who can work as independently as possible. Therapists want clients to learn the skills that they will need to move on from therapy. All leaders want to meet people's needs in such a way that those people become self-sufficient and independent. A leader's planned obsolescence means that leaders want others to be able to be leaders themselves.

It was rather sweet for Mike when Justin came back to teach. They enjoyed a different relationship. Though Mike could still advise Justin and act as somewhat of a mentor, they became more like equals who consult with one another about shared challenges. Parents experience this as their children get older, and especially as their children have children. Coaches experience this when players advance, play at higher levels, and especially when former players become coaches themselves. In all of these cases, leaders enjoy the benefits that come from good leadership and from making themselves obsolete.

A leader's humility is that person's best efforts to lovingly play God. It is knowing when to leave people to work and struggle and knowing when to intervene. It is patiently developing well-suited expectations. It is the wisdom to know when the elevator just isn't going to that floor. A leader's humility is also making every effort to become obsolete by encouraging the growth and independence of others. Finally, a leader's humility is lovingly persuading others to be humble, to be submissive, committed, and dedicated to God. Leadership's foundation is humility toward God and the leader's profound love both toward God and toward the children, students, players, employees, clients, or others that the leader is serving. In the act of playing God, leaders learn about God and become more than mere servants. Leadership provides powerful lessons about becoming like God.

SECTION ABOUT HUMILITY WHEN YOU ARE A FOLLOWER THAT SHOULD HAVE TWO STORIES BUT DOESN'T

This chapter should end with two more stories. One story should be an engaging illustration of how to be a good follower. It could be about a child, a student, a player, an employee, or someone in therapy who is willing to learn. The story should show how to be vulnerable and trusting. It should remind you that following a trustworthy leader can help you see your weakness, poverty, or Penia, but following should give you the encouragement, support, and resources or Poros that you need to grow. The story should encourage you to be a trusting child, but a child who grows to be a powerful, capable adult. It could be a story about a student struggling with new concepts, a player learning a new role or position, or an employee trusting a boss, facing a challenge, and becoming successful. It could be about a couple in therapy who have the courage to see things about themselves that they don't want to see, but who get the marriage that they had always wanted as a consequence of their brave, collaborative efforts. Finally, the story might even hint at how we can learn about God through other people. It should be a really moving story, something that encourages and inspires. You might laugh knowingly, and then toward the end you might quietly weep. Maybe.

The second story that should end this section should be a warning about trusting leaders too much. It should remind you that no person is God. It should make it clear, again in an interesting way, how you should never be submissive, committed, or dedicated to another human being in the way that you are humble toward God. It would offer a contrasting but still encouraging warning.

There are three reasons why those two fabulous stories do not appear here. The first reason is that you are probably an expert at being a good follower. If there is anything that seems to be very well taught, reinforced, illustrated, and emphasized for members of the Church of Jesus Christ of Latter-day Saints, it is the importance of being a willing and obedient follower. My guess is that you simply do not need any more stories or lessons in that.

The second reason why those stories are not here is because the second story is so hard to actually hear. You know of children who have been wise enough to act independently of their parents. You can think of students, players, employees, and perhaps even therapy clients who had to be wise enough to not accept every instruction given to them. You know of examples, but the problem is telling that kind of story. And the reason why telling that kind of story is so difficult is that it goes against so many powerful cultural teachings about trust and obedience. Let's say I tell a story about a bishop or mission president who provided guidance or direction that ward members or missionaries needed to be wise enough to ignore. Your response, I'm guessing, would be to side with the bishop or mission president. You would feel it is important to defend the leader. You would probably point out that they are doing their best. You might even argue that there is probably a misunderstanding on the part of the follower. The story might leave you believing that, even if leaders make mistakes, that should not get in the way of trustful obedience. You know that leaders are human, that they make mistakes, and that you should never trust them completely, but as soon as an example is given, you will probably resist the important warning.

The third reason why neither of those stories is here is because I think that there is a fabulous quote that reinforces the point of the second story. You may have heard this quote, but maybe not. You will not find it on a wooden plaque with a tole painting border and lettering in a Papyrus font at an LDS bookstore. It is probably not up in vinyl letters in your living room. This is not that kind of quote. In the first sentence of this quote, Brigham Young reflects on the terrible impact someone can have. He says, "What a pity it would be if we were led by one man to utter destruction!" Then Brigham asks himself this question: "Are you afraid of this?" Brigham is afraid of someone leading members of the church astray. But as he continues, Brigham says he is more afraid of something else: "I am more afraid that this people have so much confidence in their leaders that they will not inquire for themselves of God whether they are led by Him." Brigham then strongly elaborates on the danger of placing too much trust in leaders:

> I am fearful they settle down in a state of blind self-security, trusting their eternal destiny in the hands of their leaders with a reckless confidence that in itself would thwart the purposes of God in their salvation, and weaken that influence they could give to their leaders, did they know for themselves, by the revelations of Jesus, that they are led in the right way.

Brigham then challenges every member to seek to know for herself or himself: "Let every man and woman know, by the whispering of the Spirit of God to themselves, whether their leaders are walking in the path the Lord dictates, or not. This has been my exhortation continually."

This quote is better than a story. It is the fiery Brigham Young warning you and all of us to not place too much confidence in any leader. It provides wise counsel on how to be a humble, wise follower. It reinforces how your complete submission, commitment, and devotion should only be to God. Children, students, players, employees, clients, and others need the wisdom and courage to check and double check the guidance of any leader. All leaders are humans who are playing God. Not only should you never follow any leader as if that person were God, but you should carefully discern what of that leadership truly is of God and what might not be.

Mike Sanford worked for years to become a master teacher. I'm sure he made many mistakes along the way. There seem to be some common mistakes or potential mistakes any leader might make, specifically if that leader is trying to encourage the humility and obedience of others. The next chapter explores three potential errors leaders might encounter.

USING SATAN'S TOOLS TO DO GOD'S WORK **7**

THREE STORIES ABOUT FEAR, MANIPULATION, AND PRIDE

One: The Dementors. If you have read the books in J.K. Rowling's Harry Potter series or even if you've just seen the movies, you will remember the Dementors. These terrible, ghost-like creatures feed on happiness and joy. They suck all that is good out of their victims, leaving them empty shells of misery and despair. But the thing about them is that they make really good guards. The magical world's governing body, the Ministry of Magic, needs to have a prison. It needs to keep criminals inside that prison so that others can be safe. While Azkaban prison employs Dementors as guards, the escape rate is close to zero. It is hard to argue with success. Given this success, perhaps the Ministry of Magic would have always used Dementors as prison guards. But eventually the Dementors join Voldemort and the Death Eaters.

In fact, Voldemort had predicted that the Dementors would join his cause. Voldemort even says that the Dementors are his natural allies. So how is it that something so useful, powerful, and protective is also a natural ally of something so evil? This brings me to my first point: fear, though powerful and seemingly useful, is a tool that is Satan's natural ally and weapon.

Two: I worked as a missionary in the late 1980s. It was a wonderful time, filled with big testimonies and even bigger hair. But the biggest thing in missionary work back then was the *Missionary Guide*. This was the missionary training manual that came before *Preach My Gospel*. It still holds a special place for many of us who served then.

Something that was emphasized in this older manual that does not seem to be as strongly addressed in *Preach My Gospel* is avoiding manipulation. Perhaps this was just my weakness, but I seem to recall feeling called out when I read about avoiding manipulation in the *Missionary Guide*. In the section about "Asking Appropriate Questions," the guide gives effective and less effective examples. Here is the less effective example of an appropriate question: "Since you told us that you believe in Jesus Christ, how do you feel about the fact that He loves us enough to send us a prophet like Joseph Smith?" I seem to recall that when I read this question on my mission, it seemed fine to me. It seemed like it linked an investigator's belief with what was being taught. No problem, right? The manual's explanation says that in this question, "The missionaries seem to be manipulating the people to accept a belief." The section gives more examples of manipulative questions like "Since the Book of Mormon is translated by the power of God and is a second witness for Jesus Christ, how do you feel about it?" Here's a third example: "Since the prophets have spoken so strongly about every member being a missionary, I'm sure that you will help us out, won't you?"

The *Missionary Guide* uses a sample conversation with an investigator about tithing to further illustrate manipulation. The missionary begins by asking, "What do you think you should do to show your faith in God?" This question already starts to maneuver the non-member. You can feel, in the question itself, that there is only one acceptable answer. The investigator responds by saying, "I know what you're trying to say, but right now feeding my family is more important to me than donating money to the Church." This is a remarkably clear and honest statement. The missionary does not seem to genuinely acknowledge what is being said. Instead, the missionary in the example says, "We understand your concern, but what did we just read in the Bible about the blessings that would come to those who pay tithing?" Here again the missionary forces the investigator to agree. Not agreeing is denying the Bible. But the investigator will not be pushed. The investigator says, "I need money now, not 'blessings' later." This reply shows that this is a debate or a competition. The example ends with the missionary snapping back, "Do you think the Lord knows that?" In this and in other examples, the *Missionary Guide* demonstrates that missionaries like this are pushy, disrespectful, and manipulative.

Manipulation seems like it could be a very useful and

powerful way of leading people to do good things. If it is so useful and powerful, why would the *Missionary Guide* warn so often against it? This brings me to my second point: manipulation, though powerful and seemingly useful, is also a tool that is Satan's natural weapon.

Three: She seems like a very good teacher. If you were one of the parents of the girls in this teacher's select group of students, her "set," you would probably feel lucky. The teacher spends time outside of class with these students, taking them to museums and cultural events. She invites them to her home. She is training her "set" of ten-year-old girls to be cultured, sophisticated women. This teacher, Miss Brodie, lost a man she loved in the Great War, and now, in the 1930s in Scotland, she feels that her vocation, her life's calling, is educating these girls.

The phrase that Miss Brodie uses to describe the girls in her group is that they are the "crème de la crème." This phrase is used early in Muriel Spark's novel *The Prime of Miss Jean Brodie*. It is repeated several times. Miss Brodie wants the girls to feel special and see themselves as set apart from the average girls at the school. When Miss Brodie is concerned about one of the girls, she says that she's afraid the girl will never be a part of "life's élite or, as one might say, the crème de la crème."

There are a couple of other things that Miss Brodie does to urge the girls of her set to see themselves as special. Besides calling them the crème de la crème, Miss Brodie encourages them to be special and different by avoiding "team spirit." The school where Miss Brodie teaches has teams like the house system in the

Harry Potter books. The girls in Miss Brodie's set do not participate in these teams. In fact, Miss Brodie strongly warns against this sort of team spirit. She says that "team spirit" makes the girls less like individuals, less heroic, and less noble. She tells them that great women like Florence Nightingale, Cleopatra, Helen of Troy, and the Queen of England did not have team spirit. Team spirit is beneath them. Team spirit is what extras in a great play have. A play's star does not have team spirit.

Miss Brodie wants the girls of her set to see themselves as the stars of life's plays and events, not as mere supporting cast members. She conveys to them that she is in a special time in her life, and she is a special person helping them be their best. She even tells the girls that she has sacrificed personal joy and satisfaction to follow her mission of properly educating them.

Besides warning the girls against the dangers of "team spirit" and telling them that they are getting the best Miss Brodie has to offer, she does something else to help her set feel special. One day, some years after the girls of her set had left her class, Miss Brodie has them over to her house again. During this visit, Miss Brodie tells the girls that "she did not think much of her new pupils' potentialities." The narrator explains that this discussion "bound her set together more than ever and made them feel chosen." This is a closely knit, bonded group of girls who feel special, different, and above other girls. They are the crème de la crème.

So, given what has been explained about Miss Brodie and her set, why is this a problem? Isn't it good to encourage girls like this? Isn't it helpful for them to feel connected to their group?

And isn't it important that they feel special? This brings me to my third point: pride, especially an "us-versus-them" mentality that encourages people to see themselves as better than others, though powerful and seemingly useful, is a tool that is Satan's natural weapon.

What is "pride," what exactly is an "us-versus-them" mentality, and how are these Satan's natural weapons? How might pride, manipulation, and fear be approaches you should avoid? Why is it particularly important that you avoid using fear, manipulation, and pride when you are a parent, teacher, coach, boss, therapist, or any other leader? Why exactly are fear, manipulation, and pride Satan's tools?

THE DICTATORSHIP OF PRIDE

I will start by talking about the third tool I mentioned, which is pride. To understand what I mean by pride here and to understand why it is Satan's natural tool, imagine England during World War II. The country has been devastated by German bombing. Not only have thousands been killed, but thousands more are missing or wounded. Able-bodied men are off fighting. The whole world is at war, and that war has created almost overwhelming sorrow and despair. One could easily wonder, "where is God during this dark hour?"

It is in the midst of the war that C.S. Lewis gave some lectures. The lectures were not off in a college or in an auditorium. Instead, Lewis gave them on the radio. The purpose of the lectures was to lift the spirits of the downtrodden British citizens.

Another purpose of the talks was to explain Christianity. At a time when people could naturally question their faith in God, Lewis went on the radio to explain and to reinforce that faith. Lewis could not serve as a soldier, but he believed that his efforts could still make a positive difference.

After the war, Lewis' lectures where edited, revised, and published under the title *Mere Christianity*. In the lectures and book, Lewis starts by talking about belief, faith, and God. He speaks clearly and movingly about Christ and His Atonement. The second part of the book examines Christian behavior. It is in this section that Lewis describes "The Great Sin." For Lewis, that great sin is pride. Much of President Benson's influential talk about pride echoes what Lewis said.

Lewis warns that "pride can often be used to beat down the simpler vices." Lewis gives an example of a teacher who flatters a student and appeals to that student's pride in order to make the student behave properly. A teacher might say, "you don't want to be that kind of student." A parent might say, "remember who you are" before a teenager goes out with friends. If the "who you are" is someone better, higher, or superior to others, then this parent is using pride to flatter and to maneuver the teenager into making good choices. A church leader might talk about children, youth, or other church members as special, as chosen, or as a "royal generation" to get those people to behave in a particular manner. Lewis says that "many a man has overcome cowardice, or lust, or ill-temper, by learning to think that they are beneath his dignity—that is, by Pride." Miss Brodie uses similar pride to train her set to be educated, cultured, sophisticated, and above others.

Perhaps you would say that this isn't so bad. Perhaps a little bit of talk about being special or chosen is okay, especially if it produces good results. After Lewis says that some people have overcome cowardice, lust, or anger by pride, he says this: "the devil laughs." Why would Satan laugh? Lewis says that Satan is happy to have people be brave, sexually pure, and self-controlled, if, all the while, Satan is "setting up in you the Dictatorship of Pride." Pride is a much more serious sin than mere disobedience. When he says that Satan is okay with you avoiding little sins if he can get you involved in a more serious sin, Lewis says that Satan is happy to cure your acne if he can give you cancer.

What does Lewis mean by the Dictatorship of Pride? Why would pride be cancer but cowardice, lust, and a lack of self-control are merely acne? The dictatorship of pride is when pride dominates how you think and act. Pride controls how you see others and even God. Pride, as mentioned earlier, is seeing other people and seeing God as the enemy. When you see others as the enemy or when you see them as lower than you or beneath you, then that view filters everything. With this filter of pride in place, Satan really does control your thoughts, feelings, and behaviors. Lewis says that pride is spiritual cancer because "it eats up the very possibility of love, or contentment, or even common sense." You cannot love people you look down on. You cannot really listen to them or feel connected to them. You can never find contentment when you are constantly competing with others. You cannot find peace if you are always proving to others and yourself and God that you are better than others. Finally, pride makes it impossible for you to be at-one with either God or God's other children. This truly is the anti-God state.

Miss Brodie used pride to try to mold her students into what she wanted them to be. She got them to generally do well in school and to develop sophisticated manners and tastes. But she also put them in competition with everyone else. Because of her influence, they had to remind themselves, prove to themselves, prove to others, and prove to Miss Brodie that they were the crème de la crème. And they had to prove it constantly, all of the time, every day. Miss Brodie's set developed an "us-versus-them" mentality. This mentality kept them from being vulnerable. It prevented them from enjoying a healthy sense of belonging. They were too busy proving that they were special to enjoy any genuine connection with others.

There are two more dangers in the Dictatorship of Pride. If you feel you are special or chosen, you believe God is partial and biased. You believe God plays favorites. Since you are chosen, you will judge others in contrast to you. Your righteousness will be the measuring stick you use to look at others. Your righteousness will be the measuring stick you use to look down on others. In fact, using your righteousness, or what you believe is your righteousness, as the measuring stick you use to judge others is what the term "self-righteous" means.

Let's think about one more consequence that comes with the Dictatorship of Pride. Since you are mortal, what will inevitably happen? You will make a mistake. When you make a mistake, and especially if you happen to make what feels like a serious mistake, you will suddenly feel like a fraud. You will feel like you have fallen from your lofty, elevated place. You will probably feel like you have fallen below those you once looked down upon. You might see yourself as someone who looks strong or righteous or virtuous on the outside, but who is empty and rotten in the middle. The Dictatorship of Pride allows for no middle ground. Under the Dictatorship of Pride, there is no place to be a normal and flawed yet growing child of God.

THE LORD'S COMMITMENT TO AGENCY AND "WITHOUT COMPULSORY MEANS"

Part of what makes pride and flattery so dangerous are how effective they seem to be. Manipulation and fear can also seem very effective and harmless. But manipulation and fear are also Satan's natural tools. Instead of moving people or persuading people to move toward Christ, manipulation and fear more often push people away.

To hear the difference between Satan's manipulation and how the Lord would have the work done, we can again return to the *Missionary Guide*. The manipulative question was: "Since you told us that you believe in Jesus Christ, how do you feel about the fact that He loves us enough to send us a prophet like Joseph Smith?" The *Missionary Guide* suggests this as an alternative: "How do you feel about Joseph Smith as a prophet of God?" Not only is this question simpler, but it makes it easier for someone to be honest about their feelings and impressions. The *Missionary Guide* also provides an alternative to this manipulative question: "Since the Book of Mormon is translated by the power of God and is a second witness for Jesus Christ, how do you feel about it?" The open, non-manipulative question is simply, "From what we have said, what do you understand the Book of Mormon to be?" In both alternative questions, the person is not being maneuvered or manipulated into a response. The person is free to express what is actually in their mind and heart. Notice how the manipulative questions make you feel closed in and claustrophobic; the non-manipulative one makes you feel free.

The *Missionary Guide* provides an alternative to the manipulative line of questioning about tithing. The missionary does not deny or step around the person's concern about paying tithing. Instead of saying, "What do you think you should do to show your faith in God?," the missionary says, "I can appreciate your concern," followed by "In view of what we've been reading, what do you think you could do to solve the problem?" With this question, the missionary invites the person to find their own answer for the situation. Yes, the missionary invites the person to seek an answer with the scriptures, with what has been read, but the missionary does not force the person into an answer. It is much easier to imagine a person saying, "I don't know" or "I'm just not sure that is the right thing for me right now."

In the example in the *Missionary Guide*, the investigator concludes that this is a trial of faith and then expresses faith that God will support the family as they pay tithing. That is a positive outcome in the view of most missionaries, but there is more going on here. When the missionary encourages the investigator to think about ways to resolve the concern by themselves, the missionary does something mentioned in the last chapter: the missionary is making herself or himself obsolete. The missionary encourages the independence of the investigator. To put it another way, the missionary is encouraging the investigator to not need the missionaries and to instead look to the scriptures and their own efforts to find answers.

Manipulation encourages dependence, and this means that those who manipulate must continue to manipulate in order to keep people in line. Those who manipulate become a powerful force in people's lives. Tragically, that power replaces the whisperings of the Holy Ghost. In this way, those who manipulate take a place that should be God's place in the lives of others. Manipulation is Satan's tool because it, like Satan, takes a place that only God should have.

A quote and a scripture come to mind when I think of God's power. God does not influence us by manipulation. Elder Neal Maxwell said this in his BYU devotional about patience: "My brothers and sisters, the longer I examine the gospel of Jesus Christ, the more I understand that the Lord's commitment to free agency is very deep—indeed, much deeper than is our own." Elder Maxwell expresses how important it is for God that all of God's children are free. Finally, to give a sense of how those who lead and serve in God's way avoid manipulation, there is the last verse of Doctrine and Covenants section 124. In this verse, the

Lord promises blessings to those who influence others in God's way. Those people are promised constant help and companionship from the Holy Ghost as well as eternal dominion and power. Speaking of that power, the verse promises, "and without compulsory means it shall flow unto thee forever and ever." Those who manipulate seek to coerce and control. Those who lead in God's way encourage others to be free, to be independent, and to trust God. As they encourage the best in others and as they encourage others to be submissive, committed, and dedicated only to God, their influence and power flow through them freely and effortlessly.

THE LORD HATH NOT GIVEN US THE SPIRIT OF FEAR

Manipulation and pride are Satan's tools. They are tools that replace God's loving power. The third member of this unholy trinity is fear, and I don't know what else needs to be said after just mentioning in the section title Paul's teaching to Timothy that God has not given us the spirit of fear. For Paul, the opposite of fear is power, love, and a sound mind. The only thing I might add is that fear, manipulation, and pride all seem like Satan's opposites for the powerful virtues of faith, hope, and charity. Satan's counterfeits seem alluringly useful and effective. In reality, fear, manipulation, and pride lead others away from God, but faith, hope, and charity encourage people to say freely and with their whole being, "You are the Lord my God."

Freedom and healthy connection with others are the

opposites of fear, manipulation, and pride's competitive "us-ver-sus-them" alternatives. We aspire to enjoy a healthy connection with others, including those who might see things quite differently than we do. The next chapter examines how humility helps you enjoy connections and discussions precisely with those who see things differently.

HUMILITY IN TALKING **8** ABOUT POLITICS

SAME PLANET/DIFFERENT WORLDS: TWO STORIES

My wife and I have a favorite Mexican restaurant in town. On Tuesdays they do Taco Tuesday. When she orders her four tacos, she always requests cilantro. I ask the kind server to prepare my tacos without cilantro because, as all reasonable people know, cilantro is a weed that Satan uses to afflict and torment us in this fallen world. Okay, so that last part isn't exactly true, but if you, like me, don't like cilantro, then you would agree that it ruins otherwise tasty tacos. I hate to start with such a hot-button topic right off. You can tell that this chapter is really going to dive into deep controversies if we are starting with cilantro. Yep, it's gonna get intense! And now, to make it worse, I'm going to tell you that I'm leaving the cilantro controversy until later in the chapter. If you have already thrown the book across the room because of this bold, first paragraph, please pick it up and keep reading. If you were using an electronic device to read this, hopefully that thing isn't broken.

In 1989 I was living in a neighborhood in Santiago, Chile, while serving as a missionary. My companion and I lived with a family who were longtime church members. They had lived in that neighborhood for many years. At the same time, we were teaching a man who lived nearby. While the man we were teaching and the family we stayed with lived close, they had very different experiences of an important historical event. That event was the 1973 coup. During this coup, Chile's military overthrew the democratically elected government of Salvador Allende, a socialist with ties to Cuba.

Before my mission, I didn't know anything about the 1973 change in government. I learned a lot while serving there. The family that I lived with, the Moyas, acknowledged that the military rounded up and killed lots of people. Of course that was terrible, but their experience was that just before the military stepped in, there was chaos and misery. People did not feel safe. There were also very long lines for food, and the economy had crumbled. Finally, the Moyas told me that they had worked hard for many years and had bought two homes. They wanted to provide for their children, and they wanted to give them places to live. Under the socialist leadership, the government was threatening to take some of their property, including their second home. When asked about the coup, the Moya family was grateful that the military had restored order. In their eyes, the thousands of people tortured and killed by the military were part of a terrible price paid to restore order.

Nothing could be further from the Moya's experience than Tito's experience. Tito, the man we were teaching at the time, saw firsthand the military's brutality. He, his family, and family friends were victims of the military round-up, with people close to him arrested, jailed, beaten, and killed with little or no evidence of wrongdoing and without a trial. Tito's family suspected what was later revealed to be true: that the United States government had spent millions of dollars to weaken Chile's economy. The US CIA had supported groups that created the chaos that the Moyas found so terrible. That chaos provided the opportunity for the coup. While the coup brought the structure and order that the Moyas appreciated, it also brought brutal oppression, torture, and death for Tito's family and friends.

Tito and the Moyas lived on the same planet, in the same neighborhood, but in different worlds. Imagine them sitting in church together. Sure, it might be fine when everyone is only talking about faith, repentance, baptism, and the Holy Ghost, but once politics is even hinted at, these people are about as far apart as you could imagine.

Members of the Church of Jesus Christ of Latter-day Saints in Chile, and I add all over the world, can be sharply divided by politics. We are members of the church and we live on the same planet, but it can feel like we live in completely different worlds. The normal way to deal with this division is to simply avoid the topic. But I think we can do better. I believe that with some knowledge and some humility we can talk about politics. In fact, I think we can have valuable, productive conversations about politics. I think that the church, that Zion, will be better as we have those conversations.

HUMILITY, KNOWLEDGE, AND JONATHAN HAIDT

From what you have read in this book so far, you can probably see how humility is important for conversations about politics. Humility is especially important when you have political conversations with people who have very different views and experiences. If Tito and the Moyas were to talk productively about politics, it would be important that they not see each other as enemies. As has been stated many times, seeing others as the enemy is how C.S. Lewis and President Benson define pride. These Chileans would have to decide to see each other as friends and as good people with something valuable to add to the conversation.

But there is something else that might help them and that might help us as we talk about politics. That something else is knowledge. The knowledge I mean includes some insights developed by Jonathan Haidt. Haidt has spent many years studying morality, and he has developed some remarkable conclusions. One conclusion is that conservatives and liberals view right and wrong differently. When you understand those differences, you can see better how others view the world.

After studying people around the world, Haidt found that there are five parts of morality. The first part is harm. When you see someone harming someone else, it feels wrong. All of us naturally come to the aid of a crying child, a hurt animal, a grieving elderly woman. Our hearts go out to the hungry, the naked, the poor, and the needy.

The second part of morality is justice. It feels wrong to you when you see people treated unfairly, and it feels good when you see the rules apply evenly to everyone. But this might surprise you: justice can be different if you are conservative or liberal. Before I describe this, I want to emphasize that Jonathan Haidt uses the labels "liberal" and "conservative" to describe groups of people. He says that most people fall between these two ends. Most people are a mixture of conservative and liberal. I also want to add that if you already don't like the word "liberal" or the word "conservative," if even reading those words reminds you of political enemies, then please keep reading. This section is for you.

Liberals and conservatives, according to Haidt, see justice differently. When conservatives think about justice, they emphasize how people should get what they deserve. If you work hard, you should get the rewards. If you slack off, you should not take from those who were diligent. A great scripture story about conservative justice is the servants who are given the talents. In the story, the servants who wisely and diligently invested the talents were rewarded. The lazy servant was condemned. Justice was properly served.

Liberals also believe in justice, but for liberals, justice is ending the unfairness we see around us. When liberals think about justice, they think about the naked, hungry, cold, alone, and suffering. Liberals see great inequality as wrong. When a liberal sees someone with millions and millions of dollars drive by a homeless person living on the street, that strikes a liberal as deeply, morally wrong. For liberals, inequality is a terrible sin; it is iniquity. When liberals read the scriptures, they feel strongly about King Benjamin's words about helping beggars and Christ's words about what we have done for the needy we have done or not done for Him.

Okay, before we go on, let's take a moment to go wow. Wow! Isn't that amazing! Both of those are very, very good ideas about justice. It is right to get what you deserve. It can also feel really wrong for lazy people to take from those who work. But it also seems really wrong to have some people with so much while others suffer. Fairness and justice turn out to be more complicated than you might think. And let me remind you again that most people are a mixture of conservative and liberal. One of these ideas about justice might seem stronger or more important to you. That means you lean to that side. You might be right in the middle, or you might lean slightly or even strongly to one side.

The difference between the way liberals see justice and fairness and the way conservatives see them is just one difference. Other differences come with Haidt's ideas about the other three parts of morality. Those three parts are respect for authority, group loyalty, and respect for taboos.

Respect for authority is exactly what it sounds like. Conservatives, according to Haidt's research, have a strong sense of respect for authority. Conservatives feel it is wrong and disloyal to be negative or cynical about leaders. Conservatives not only give authority figures the benefit of the doubt, but they are willing to trust them in spite of uncertainty. Conservatives feel strongly connected to scriptures about how God speaks through leaders and authorities, and how we can trust those leaders. Conservatives may not feel really excited or may have even cringed at the quote from Brigham Young in chapter six where he warns about placing too much trust in leaders.

Along with respect for authority is loyalty to your group. This is another feeling that is strong for conservatives. This loyalty means commitment and devotion to the group, and it also means that disloyalty and betrayal feel deeply wrong. Conservative loyalty to the group can be found in their patriotism and in their strong connection with gratitude for being part of the only true and living church on the earth.

The final element of morality is respect for taboos. In every culture, certain things are taboo. To outsiders, those things might seem unimportant, but taboos are things that you just don't do. For Mormons, it is taboo, for example, to have sex outside of marriage, to break the Word of Wisdom, or to talk about the temple in disrespectful ways. Conservatives have a very strong sense that taboos should be respected. In other words, for conservatives, breaking and even questioning taboos can feel very wrong.

So what about liberals? If conservatives feel strongly about respecting authority, being loyal to your group, and respecting taboos, what about liberals? According to Haidt, liberals don't feel as strongly about those things. In fact, liberals can feel quite comfortable questioning authority. A liberal member of the church might have Brigham Young's quote up on a wall in the house. Liberals can also have serious questions about group loyalty. Finally, liberals may not feel nearly as strongly about certain taboos. But how does that make sense morally? For liberals, intense respect for authorities, group loyalty, and concern about taboos sound like the Pharisees. The Pharisees rejected Jesus and His teachings precisely because they saw Him as a threat to respected authorities, to group loyalty, and to their taboos. Jesus made their leaders look foolish, He praised Samaritans, He ate with the wrong people, and He questioned their many rules. Liberals connect deeply with those stories about Jesus.

For liberals, humans do their best to be good leaders, but they are still just human. Liberals would never want to mistake leaders for God, so their moral sense of respecting authority is not as high as it is for conservatives. Liberals also don't feel nearly as strongly about group loyalty. For liberals, group loyalty is too often exclusive. It can be one group claiming to be better, special, or more loved by God than another. This inequality seems deeply wrong for liberals. Liberals may not feel comfortable claiming that they are part of God's only true church upon the earth. That notion just feels like an us-versus-them approach. It can feel like pride. Liberals love the church and church members, but they would not want that love to outweigh their love for all of God's children. And just like liberals don't feel as strongly about respect for authority or group loyalty, they don't feel as strongly about respecting taboos. Liberals don't break taboos just to break them, since that would be foolish and hurtful. But liberals emphasize how oxen can be in the mire and how you should not be so concerned about counting steps on Sunday or straining gnats that you miss what is really important.

Okay, so let's just say this one more time—wow! Wow! Liberals and conservatives see the world very differently. To really bring those differences into focus, let's use an example: temple sealings for gay couples. Yep, you just read those five words correctly—temple sealings for gay couples.

First, how would conservatives view this? Can you see how they would see this as morally wrong? And why would they see it that way? I think the most fundamental reason is that conservatives view homosexual relations as wrong. Homosexual sex is taboo. For conservatives, it just seems deeply wrong. In addition, conservatives who respect authorities in the form of church leaders also respect what leaders have taught and said about marriage. It feels very morally right to conservatives that marriage is between one man and one woman. It feels right because it respects taboos and authorities. It can also feel right because it is loyal to the church, to church teachings, and to doctrine. For conservatives, there is a clear, morally right answer to this question, and that is that temple sealings for gay couples are wrong.

Can you imagine how a liberal might view temple sealings for gay couples? First, for liberals, gay people are not gay because of a sinful choice. Gay people are gay because God made them that way, and God loves them that way. Liberals do not view homosexuality or homosexual sex as taboo. In addition, liberals respect authorities but believe that God will yet reveal many great and important things pertaining to the Kingdom of God. God once banned black families from being sealed in the temple, so liberals are very open to the idea that God may one day allow gay couples to do the same. Liberals do not feel a sense of disloyalty in continuing revelation or in seeing how the church might change. But the real liberal moral center is harm. While liberals do not have the strong sense of respect for authority, group loyalty, or respect for taboos that conservatives have, they have a very strong sense that harm is deeply, deeply wrong. For liberals, the current church ban on temple sealings for gay couples is harmful. This ban tells gay couples that they are at best second-class citizens if not frankly unwanted in God's kingdom and church. It says that they are eternally flawed, broken, or God's mistake. The ban says that they are not loved like God's heterosexual children. Liberals fear that the ban may contribute to the suicide rate among gay Mormons. All of that feels deeply, deeply wrong to liberals.

And now, one more time, wow! Isn't that amazing! I hope that this example demonstrates one important thing: good, thoughtful, righteous, moral people can see things very, very differently. And good, thoughtful, righteous, and moral people can disagree. Just as the Moyas and Tito saw the Chilean coup very, very differently, so can all of us see important issues very differently.

One temptation that I'm sure you are wise enough to avoid but which I'll mention anyways is this: so which one is correct? Are liberals right or are conservatives? Of course the answer is: who is right about cilantro, me or my wife? When it comes to cilantro, we are both right and both wrong. It tastes right, great even, to my wife. To me it tastes like some sort of weed that ruins a perfectly good taco. For conservatives, temple sealings for gay couples is a concept that feels wrong. Heterosexual marriage between one man and one woman feels very, very right for conservatives. For liberals, heterosexual marriage feels morally right, but temple sealings for gay couples at least feels possible if not very, very right. In addition to temple sealings for gay couples, conservatives and liberals may also view the following ideas very differently: female priesthood ordination and the ideas that the Church of Jesus Christ of Latter-day Saints is the only true and living church upon the earth and that the Lord will never permit the President of the Church to lead you astray. These are just some places where there might be deep differences.

I said at the outset that I think that knowledge and humility are key to members of the church having political discussions over issues where we disagree. If you have not considered this before, I hope that the idea that liberals and conservatives have different views of morality provides some knowledge. I hope that it is clear that both groups include good, thoughtful, righteous, and moral people in spite of the fact that they see morality differently. Knowing this can help us recognize those differences. This knowledge might help us respect people in our lives who view morality differently. This knowledge might help us listen to others more carefully, more insightfully. It might help us avoid seeing these people as enemies as we instead see them as teammates and friends.

INSTRUMENTS OF THE LORD'S PEACE

Imagine what it would be like if every discussion about politics among church members were respectful, wise, and humble. Imagine what we might all learn from one another. Robert S. Wood provides a vision of what it might look like to have those sorts of discussions. In addition to a vision, Brother Wood, in an April 2006 General Conference talk, issues a warning. He notes that it seems like too often discussions, including political ones, are clouded by thoughtlessness and anger. He warned us to watch out for those who stir up so much anger that we cannot think straight, we cannot calmly reflect, and we lose our loving, charitable feelings toward one another. He goes on to remind us that we have made covenants with God and with each other. We have promised to bear one another's burdens and comfort those who need comfort. Given that we have made those promises to one another, Brother Wood wonders if perhaps we are breaking those promises by lapsing into bad patterns. One of those bad patterns is emphasizing and exaggerating what we see as wrong in others. Bad patterns also include reducing people who see things differently to oversimplified stereotypes.

Brother Wood doesn't mention those stereotypes specifically, but, given what we have already talked about, they are easy to predict. Liberals might accuse conservatives of being proud and exclusive. Liberals might also say that conservatives are biased and blinded by their group loyalty or respect for authority. Liberals might dismiss conservatives by calling them Pharisees.

Conservatives might question the faith or righteousness of liberals. They might claim that liberals cannot be good members of the church if they don't have the same views about authority, loyalty, and taboos that they have. Conservatives might mock the liberal desire to reduce harm and suffering. Both groups have their morality and even scriptures to back up their views, but this approach destroys the bonds of love that should tie us together as God's children and as members of the church.

Brother Wood tells a story about writing a paper for a class where he criticized someone's view. His professor said that the paper was incomplete because he had failed to respectfully understand the view he was criticizing. Perhaps the best benefit of Haidt's ideas about how liberals and conservatives view morality is that it might help us really understand how someone can see something so differently. Haidt gives us knowledge so we can be humble.

The goal that Brother Wood holds up is that, as we interact, listen, and speak humbly and with love, we will be instruments in God's hands to bring peace, light, and joy to the world.

TACOS AT THE WARD POTLUCK

I think that knowledge and humility can help us have respectful, insightful, and mutually beneficial discussions even about the most difficult issues. That said, I don't think it will always be easy. Sometimes others may not be willing to see things the way that you do. They may be very liberal or very conservative, and what they say may be very different from how you see things. I can say from my experience that this is like someone bringing tacos to the ward potluck that have tons of cilantro. Of course they didn't mean to make tacos that I find disgusting. In fact, they made tacos that they thought were delicious. What they made was meant to be good. It was meant to be a blessing to me. In a worst case scenario, they might see me take one, and after I take a bite they might immediately ask what I think. What can I say? Well, it is not too difficult to explain that they are delicious, but that I don't care for cilantro.

What do you do if you are in a class or meeting where the teacher or speaker takes a very different approach than yours? What if the lesson or talk is filled with cilantro, so to speak? Of course the clear answer for every situation is . . . I don't know. All I can suggest is that first you acknowledge the uncomfortable feelings you will have. This will strike you as wrong, and it will hurt. Remember, you didn't choose how you see things morally. Your views of morality are part of you like a taste for or against cilantro. You are neither wrong nor right to view things the way you do. You are just different from the speaker or teacher.

My second suggestion for when you get metaphorical cilantro in a church meeting is to not jump ship. I know I'm using too many metaphors, and I'm sorry, but I want to emphasize that. Please, do not leave the church. Perhaps you may feel like an outsider if you are the only one or feel like the only one who sees things the way you do. Believe me when I say that that is not the case. In addition, and this is very important, please keep this in mind: the church needs you. What I mean by that is that the church needs different points of view. Part of why that is so important is because conservatives have 20/20 vision for the blind spots of liberals, and liberals have 20/20 vision for the blind spots of conservatives. Liberals don't want to sink into chaos. Liberals don't want a world where everything you say, believe, or think must be right. They also don't want to encourage laziness or complacency, and they definitely don't want to help people in ways that actually hurt instead of help. Conservative voices provide warnings against all of those things. And conservatives don't want to fall into inappropriate respect or worship of leaders. Conservatives don't want loyalty that becomes proud bias or exclusion. They definitely don't want to be Pharisees. Liberal voices warn against all of those things. If your voice is not part of the conversation, something important is lost in Zion. Please stay.

My third suggestion is about what you should do at that moment. Here I'm really lost. Perhaps you could respectfully offer your view in a class discussion. Perhaps you might pull the speaker or teacher aside to share how you feel. Perhaps you will do nothing. You might just look for an opportunity to share or say something in the future, or you might just let it be. Here again, my best advice is to let knowledge, humility, and wisdom be your guide.

I believe that we can be instruments of the Lord's peace. I believe that when we combine knowledge with humility, we can speak productively with one another about issues where we see things differently.

The ways that you interact with others can build, lift, and encourage. We are meant to be connected to one another. In our connections, we use language and behavior to send signals to others. Those social signals and how those signals relate to modesty and humility are addressed in the next chapter.

MODESTY IS NOT THE SAME AS HUMILITY **9**

THAT GREAT TALK YOU GAVE

You have just given a talk in church. It was a really good talk. You prepared for this talk for several weeks, you have a strong testimony of the topic, and you wanted everyone to understand it better and to feel the influence of the Holy Ghost as you spoke. When you gave the talk, it came out just like you had practiced it. You felt very good when it was done. After the meeting, several people approached you to praise you for the talk you'd given. So, in this book about being more humble, what is the appropriate humble response to their praise?

Before you answer, let's think about this question in light of what has been said about humility. Imagine that someone comes up to you and says, "wow, that was an interesting talk! I had never thought about that topic in that way, and I really felt the Spirit!" If you are really submissive, committed, and dedicated to God, what is the correct response? You could say, "all of the glory be to God," but, let's face it, that sounds weird. At least it sounds weird in the Mormon culture that I've experienced. It sounds like you just scored the game-winning Superbowl touchdown. You could say that over the years, you saw your weakness, your poverty, your Penia in preparing talks and understanding the topic, but eventually your efforts and God's grace have been the resources, the Poros, that transformed your weakness into a strength. But that sounds weird too. I think what you would commonly think of as a "humble" response would be something like this: "well, I thought that the other talks were really great, I mean, I really got a lot out of them." The upside to this reply is that it is not weird like the previous options. In fact, this sounds like something you have probably heard and maybe even said yourself. The tactic avoids the praise by deflecting it to someone else. Athletes often do this, taking any praise they get for individual efforts and putting it back on the entire team and the coaches (and God, of course). But there is something off about this response. The person praising you wants to tell you something, wants to thank you for something you have given. Their praise is a gift of gratitude. Instead of accepting that gift, you deflect it or pass it along or otherwise turn it down. Here are some other common things that you could say that turn down such a gift: "Oh, well, it wasn't that great" or "the best parts were actually taken from a General Conference talk I read" or "I'm sure you could have done much better."

This highlights the problem—praise is a gift that can be

difficult to accept. The reason why it is difficult to accept is because you don't want to seem proud.

What do you think of this response: "thank you. It is a topic that means a lot to me, I worked very hard on the talk, and I'm glad you liked it and felt the Spirit." How does that response seem to you? It is honest, straightforward, and readily accepts the praise. It acknowledges the gift of gratitude that has been given. It shows that the speaker sees herself or himself as somewhat like a fluent missionary. But it can also seem too honest, too straightforward, and too willing to accept praise. It can seem proud. If nothing else, it might not seem humble.

This situation, this problem of receiving praise, brings up an important issue: modesty is not the same as humility.

MODESTY IS NOT THE SAME AS HUMILITY

To explain how modesty is not the same as humility, imagine wearing a jersey, a huge, multicolored wig, and a gigantic foam finger to church. I'm sure you have never found yourself in the pew on a Sunday morning dressed like that, but you may have spent a Saturday or two wearing those very things at a basketball, football, baseball, or soccer game or other sports event. You also know better than to wear church clothes to cheer on your favorite team. You would feel quite uncomfortable wearing the wrong things to church or a sports event. You would feel out of place; you would feel like you were sticking out instead of blending in with everyone else. Dressed like that you would probably worry that you were being a distraction. In either case you would be violating certain social expectations or norms.

If you are driving along and see a bunch of people with similar jerseys and brandishing foam fingers while walking together and talking loudly, you could probably guess the location of the stadium and the parking lot or train station. You recognize clues evident in their common dress and their behavior. You easily draw conclusions from those clues. Dress, behavior, and language send social messages. Modesty is the skill of using dress, behavior, and language to send socially appropriate messages. Modesty means knowing what to wear to church and to sporting events, how to act when you are a leader so that others trust and follow you, and what to say so that you don't sound arrogant when someone praises you.

This last point, that modesty means saying the right things so that you don't sound arrogant, is worth exploring in more depth. A modest response to praise is a response that gives others the sense that you are not self-centered, boastful, or too proud of yourself or your accomplishments. A modest person would not say, in response to the good talk mentioned earlier, "yah, that was about the best talk I've ever given, and I wish more people would have been here to hear it!" That response sounds conceited. In fact, part of the reason you might sometimes laugh at children and young people is that those people might not understand the social messages behind some language. You would probably laugh, at least to yourself, if you heard a young person say, "Did you hear my talk? I totally crushed it!" This response does not conform to social expectations, and there is a good chance that the young speaker may not realize how arrogant that person sounds.

This gets to the point of this section—modesty is not the same as humility. When the young person says, "Did you hear my talk? I totally crushed it!," that person is not modest. This language sends inappropriate social signals. The seemingly boastful response is so awkward that it is almost as if the young person suddenly threw on a jersey, wig, and foam finger right there in the church. But even that boastful response may not seem boastful in other circumstances. A young person who comes home to tell parents that they "totally crushed the chemistry exam" or who comes into the house happy that they had "totally crushed changing the oil in the van" is saying something that is socially acceptable.

Modesty is a good thing. It is good to know what to say and how to behave so that you send appropriates social signals. It can be a challenge when you don't know what to say or do. It can make you feel awkward and out-of-place. But being awkward and not knowing how to always send appropriate social messages is not evil. When the young person above said something that sounded arrogant, that person was not breaking a commandment. That young person was not violating a covenant. In fact, when you think about it, wearing a jersey, wig, and foam finger to church is distracting, but it isn't morally wrong. You are not evil because you send awkward social messages.

There is another level to modesty as well. Not only are you not evil if you send poorly timed social messages, but if you happen to always send just the right social messages, that does not necessarily mean you are good. Someone might know just what to wear, just what to say, and just how to act to send all of the right social messages, but that person might be manipulative, cruel, dishonest, or darkly hypocritical. Someone can be modest but not humble.

This highlights the important difference between modesty, or the skill for sending appropriate social messages, and humility, or your submission, commitment, and devotion to God and your loving, wise commitment to others. Humility is saying with your being, "You are the Lord my God." Modesty is saying the right things in social settings. Humility is genuine friendship with others, wisely confronting when it is called for (Kent) while still being willing to forgive and not hold grudges (Cordelia). Humility is using the language of request and respect in interacting with equals. Modesty helps you fit in socially and to interact comfortably with others. Humility is using all of your resources to do God's work in God's way. Humility is combining wisdom and patience to have open, honest discussions with people who view things differently. Modesty is the skill for not seeming arrogant during those discussions. Humility is a central quality in Christ's character. As you become more humble, you become more like Him. Modesty is . . . not all that. Yes, work on being modest, since it is a valuable skill to have, but modesty should never be mistaken for humility.

Before I finish this discussion of modesty and its relationship with humility, I will mention another side of modesty. The place that you might most often hear the word "modesty" in the culture that often surrounds members of the Church of Jesus Christ of Latter-day Saints has to do almost exclusively with women. Modesty here is about social signals women send with the way that they behave, speak, and especially dress. The central concern in those discussions is the social signals women send about their sexual availability. This book's focus is not on that type of modesty. While that modesty or lack thereof, again, is not this book's focus, a woman's modesty in her dress, behavior, and language is at best a good skill to have, but that modesty tells you little or nothing about her actual goodness or her genuine humility.

A "HUMBLE" BACKGROUND

To round off the book's discussion of humility, I want to point out that sometimes "humble" is a nice word or euphemism for poor. An example is found in these sentences from a General Conference talk: "in the sacred sealing room, the eternal marriage ordinance is the same for everyone. I love the fact that the couple from the humblest background and the couple from the wealthiest background have exactly the same experience." "Humble" here is the opposite of wealthy. This is an especially convenient word if the culture seems to value wealth and if it is suspicious or embarrassed by poverty. Calling people "humble" can just sound nicer than calling them poor. But here again, being poor when it comes to wealth and the privileges that come with money is not the same as being submissive, committed, or dedicated to God. Poor people might avoid the temptation to trust their wealth or talents instead of trusting God, but they might not. Poor people might be just as greedy, envious, and selfish as the rich. Poor people might see God and others as the enemy just as often and just as strongly as the rich. The poor and the rich have the same temple experience, make the same covenants, and have the same loving God. It does sound kind and polite to call a poor background a "humble" one, but using humility in that way should not be mistaken for the humility that has to do with your relationship with God or your relationship with others.

One way to understand humility's nature is to think of a very common diagram that members of the Church of Jesus Christ of Latter-day Saints often use to describe pride. The next chapter is an examination of the "pride cycle."

A REVISED PRIDE CYCLE 10

TWO DIAGRAMS

One common way that members of the Church of Jesus Christ of Latter-day Saints talk about pride is in the "pride cycle." We often think of the "pride cycle" in conjunction with the Book of Mormon. The cycle goes like this: bad things, like destruction and suffering, come when people turn away from God (see figure 1). This is at the bottom of the diagram. In response to those tragedies, people humble themselves and repent. Humility and repentance bring righteousness and prosperity. It is called the "pride cycle" because, in response to prosperity, people turn their backs on God, falling into pride and wickedness. Prosperous people rely upon themselves instead of God, they chalk up their success to their own efforts instead of God's gracious providence, and they turn away from God. They end up seeing God as the enemy, which is the enmity at pride's core. Pride and wickedness inevitably lead to destruction and suffering, and the cycle begins

RIGHTEOUSNESS
AND PROSPERITY

HUMILITY AND
REPENTANCE

PRIDE AND
WICKEDNESS

DESTRUCTION
AND SUFFERING

▲ **FIGURE 1**   THE PRIDE CYCLE   ▶ **FIGURE 2**   REVISED PRIDE CYCLE

all over again. Mormon seems to have such a cycle in mind in the conclusions he draws as recorded in Helaman chapter twelve.

This version of the "pride cycle" is very useful. It illustrates how prosperity can entice you to turn away or to at least set aside God when that help no longer seems pressing. It is a powerful warning against complacency and against relying too much on yourself and your capacities. One potential problem with this illustration is that it makes pride and wickedness seem unavoidable. The cycle does not visually allow for alternatives to falling right back into wickedness and pride as a natural outcome of prosperity. In this cycle, prosperity always leads to pride.

Figure 2 gives another version of the pride cycle. At first, it might seem overly complicated, but it is actually rather simple.

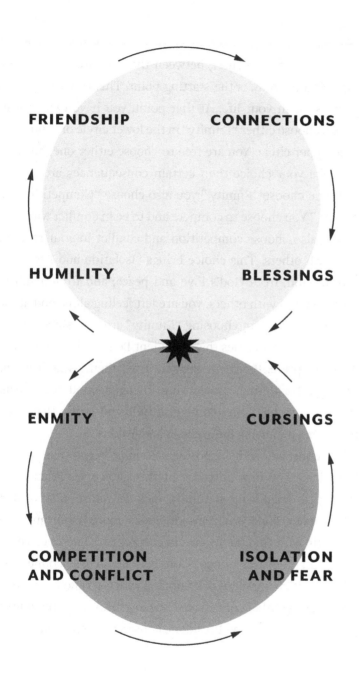

FRIENDSHIP   CONNECTIONS

HUMILITY   BLESSINGS

ENMITY   CURSINGS

COMPETITION   ISOLATION
AND CONFLICT   AND FEAR

The star at the center, between the two circles and at the center of a figure 8, is the starting point. This is where you are at any point in your life. At that point, you have two choices. You can choose either "Enmity" in the lower circle or "Humility" in the upper circle. You are free to choose either one, but once you make your choice then certain consequences are inevitable. If you choose "Enmity," you also choose "Competition and Conflict." You choose to compete and to be in conflict with God, but you also choose competition and conflict in your relationships with others. This choice brings "Isolation and Fear." Cut off from God, from God's love and peace, and from a satisfying connection with others, you are left feeling alone and afraid. The final outcome of choosing "Enmity" are "Cursings." Those cursings are the miseries that President Benson described in his talk about pride. President Benson listed them as faultfinding, gossiping, backbiting, murmuring, living beyond our means, envying, coveting, withholding gratitude and praise that might lift another, and being unforgiving and jealous.

In contrast with choosing "Enmity," you can choose "Humility." The first outcome of this choice is "Friendship." While that friendship naturally includes close relationships with people around you, it also includes, more importantly, the friendship with God mentioned in chapter two. Such a closeness with God and others brings "Connections." These connections include a satisfying sense of belonging with God and with others. The "Blessings" that come from choosing "Humility" include the opposites of everything President Benson warned about: seeing the good in others, sharing encouraging words, lifting others, patience, self-control, gratitude for what you have, being open and free in your praise and love for others, readily forgiving, and living free of jealousy. Humility's blessings seem to include being filled with faith, hope, and Christ's pure love. One final note about the diagram is that "Blessings" as well as "Cursings" bring you back to the center, to the choosing point.

This diagram can still be used to illustrate what seems all-too-common in the Book of Mormon. Sadly, soon after people choose humility and enjoy the blessings that come from such a choice, they return to the choosing point where they turn from God and choose enmity. We can easily see people in the Book of Mormon making their way around this diagram.

THE VICIOUS CYCLE AND THE VIRTUOUS CYCLE

One advantage to this diagram is that it shows how both the "proud," or those who choose enmity toward God, and the humble can become "stronger and stronger" in their enmity or humility. Those who choose to see God as the enemy and who then experience the unavoidable "cursings" can choose to turn away and to hate God even more. They can blame God and others for their misery, finding even greater "Competition and Conflict." When they feel more and more "Isolation and Fear," they may choose more anger as both a weapon and as a way to temporarily numb their painful feelings. They become "hardened in their hearts" toward God and others, losing any kindness, softness, or openness they may have once had. This diagram illustrates how choosing "Enmity" can lead to a vicious repetition and reinforcement of bad choices and their terrible outcomes.

Fortunately, the diagram also shows the opposite. Those who choose "Humility" may start to enjoy the consequences of that choice and its blessings, and this might persuade them to continue to choose such humility. "Friendship" with God and others becomes stronger and stronger as does their satisfying and fulfilling sense of connection with others. Those who are humble become firmer and firmer in their confidence in God, in God's plan, timing, and promises. Choosing humility becomes easier and easier until it is in their very nature to make that choice. The humble can continue to make choices in a virtuous cycle. It may be worthwhile to re-read the first chapter of Alma with this diagram.

Not only does this diagram illustrate how people can become "stronger and stronger" in either humility or enmity, it also shows that enmity and wickedness are not unavoidable. "Blessings," including prosperity, do not have to lead to wickedness and destruction. Blessings can just as easily lead to more humility. What the diagram emphasizes is that you get to choose. But the diagram also shows how you must choose. Finally, what I like most about the diagram, personally, is that it leads me to ask this question: "God, how can I be more humble?" I'm invited to see how I can be more submissive, more committed, and more dedicated to the Lord. I consider how I can choose friendship with God and with others. I also use the diagram to see where I am proud. I ask myself where I am choosing enmity or where

I am seeing God and others as the enemy. This diagram provides an interesting illustration of what humility is, what it leads to, what pride is, and what are its outcomes.

The diagram illustrates a choice between humility and pride, but I believe that there is a bit more to the "comparison and conflict" that follow "enmity." Comparison and conflict are so common in most of our lives that they seem to be natural. Perhaps I'm just too much of a "natural man" and enemy to God and others, but I frequently compare myself with others. The next chapter examines why comparison is so common. The chapter explicitly states who is responsible for so much comparison. You might be thinking that the devil is responsible for all of this "natural man" comparison, but, spoiler alert, it turns out that all of this comparison goes back to a guy named Doug.

PRACTICAL HUMILITY **11**
IN DAILY LIFE

THE DOUG DILEMMA,
OR WHY I JUDGE AND COMPARE

Three pre-historic hunters crawl slowly through the tall grass. Their total focus is on the wooly mastodon that is almost within spear-throwing distance. This massive animal will feed the hunters and the other members of their group for a few days. On the signal, all three hunters in unison hurl their flint-topped spears. Not enough of the spears hit the mark to drop it immediately, so they will need to pursue the animal for many hours. They will return to their group with the animal, but it will be later than anyone would hope. And it is all Doug's fault. There are supposed to be four pre-historic hunters crawling slowly through the tall grass, and four hunters hurling spears, but Doug fell asleep a mile or so back, and when they tried to wake him he got crabby and told them to just go themselves and he'd catch up later. They could all be on their way back to camp now, but no, Doug, as usual, is making them all do extra work because he's stubborn, lazy, and unreliable. The three valiant hunters will slay the mighty mastodon and take it back to the group, but you know that they are going to talk trash about Doug the entire time.

In the college classes that I teach, I would love to do more group projects. Group projects can create better learning for everyone. Just like four hunters can catch much more than one hunter acting alone, so group projects can produce much more learning than the singular studying of a solitary student. But the reason I don't give a lot of group projects, unless I want students to hate me, is because of the Dougs of the world. Students dread group projects because it is awful to have group members not doing their part. The Dougs don't make the contributions that the group wants, and they make it difficult for everyone to do their part. One Doug harms the morale of everyone in the group. Each of the three mastodon hunters is probably questioning, at least to herself or himself, why they should work so hard when Doug is not only sleeping but will eventually get some of the mastodon meat.

There is a specific term for the Dougs in group projects. That term is "free rider." Doug rides along with the group without paying or doing all of his part. The fancy term for what I call the "Doug Dilemma" is the "free rider problem." This is actually a rather huge problem. Once humans start to form groups, like the pre-historic mastodon hunters, those groups must deal with the free rider problem. What can our hunter-gatherers do about their free rider problem? How do they solve a problem like Doug? They could kill him. Killing Doug would solve part of the problem by eliminating his bad influence on the group. At least people might stop questioning why they should work so hard while the lazy Dougs ride for free. But killing Doug is not a great solution. Killing Doug means one less person to help out. Also, once you start killing free riders, it could be way too easy to kill anyone in the group who even seems to slack off. Killing Dougs is just a path we don't want to go down.

The other thing you can do to address the Doug Dilemma is exactly what the other three hunters did—talk trash about Doug. Talking trash about Doug actually turns out to be a pretty good solution. It avoids the moral unpleasantness of killing him, but it still punishes him. When the hunters get back to their group, everyone will find out how Doug slacked off and didn't do his part. Doug will end up with a bad reputation. Doug's bad reputation will mean a lower group status. That low status will mean that Doug will probably get the least desirable portions of food and other group products. In the long run, if Doug has children, he will probably not have them with a high-status, well-respected partner. Doug will not enjoy the benefits of full contribution to the group because he is not fully contributing and because everyone knows it.

We can also be optimistic about how the trash talking might impact Doug. Doug will probably not like it, and he might change his ways. He might start doing his part. He might double his efforts to contribute to the group. If a chastened Doug changes his ways, that would be great for the group—he can now contribute and everyone in the group can learn a valuable anti-free riding lesson.

I hate to say it this way but trash talking about Doug helps the group. It is not a pretty solution, but it is a useful solution to the Doug Dilemma or free rider problem. Yes, it actively shames Doug, but that is because Doug's slacking off is a powerful threat to the group. One Doug pulls the entire group down. If you still need a reminder of how bad the free rider problem is, remember how much you dislike group projects. If you could effectively collaborate with others, you could get a lot out of group projects. The reason that you don't enjoy and benefit from group projects is Dougs. Talking trash about Doug warns the whole group to not act like him. The trash talking might persuade Doug to change, but even if it doesn't, it still helps the group isolate and minimize his negative influence.

There are a few more things to note about this group and its attempt to solve a problem like Doug. Once people in the group talk trash about Doug, they are judging him. Judging Doug invites group members to judge other members. As they judge, they will notice hard working group members who make great contributions. We will call a hard-working group contributor Beverly. Once group members judge others, they will turn their judgement on themselves. Now, before we rush to the conclusion that all of this judgement is bad, keep in mind that there has to be judgement to solve the free rider problem. Each member needs to see Doug's slacking. They also need to see how Doug's slacking harms the group. Each member needs to see how Beverly's hard work benefits everyone. And we want the Dougs to understand their slacking and how it harms the group just like we want the Beverlies to understand and value their contributions. Everyone in the group will compare the Beverlies to the Dougs. We also want the Dougs and Beverlies to compare themselves to each other. Finally, the Beverlies will be respected and valued over the Dougs. They will have a higher status because of what they contribute. And there we go—to solve the free rider problem, the problem that can destroy any group, we now have a group with high status and low status members and a group where everyone judges and compares everyone.

I know that this sounds like a terrible group. It sounds like the "natural man" struggling, judging, comparing, and competing in the lone and dreary world. For the group to survive, everyone must do their part. This will mean that there are lots of expectations and demands placed on everyone. Some group members will find these expectations overwhelming. Group members may feel like they are "not enough" and that they cannot live up to their group's expectations. This is an awful feeling. It is also an inevitable outcome of trash talking as a solution to the free rider problem. The group will be okay if the Dougs feel pressured to do more and to live up to higher group expectations. There is no way to only place that pressure on the Dougs and not on the Beverlies and on everyone else.

It is my view that we are all in groups like this. Society is a group like this. Your ward or branch is a group like this. Even your family is a group like this. To illustrate what it is like in groups like these, here are two quick experiences.

A few weeks ago, my daughter and her husband secured a contract for their first house. They are twentysomethings with a son who is almost two. My son-in-law and daughter have great jobs. Combined, they make twice as much money as I do. We went to see their new home. It is in a really nice neighborhood—tree lined streets, a pond with a small baseball diamond nearby, a white gazebo with white blossoming azaleas. Lovely, lovely, lovely. Their house has large windows and new hardwood floors. When I walked into their home for the first time, one of the feelings I had was jealousy.

Last Sunday, we got a new Bishop. He teaches at the same university where I work. He is in the business school, and doubtlessly makes quite a bit more money than I do. He is also one of the finest men I know. He worked with my sons in the Young Men program, and his service and influence have been a blessing to them and to me. And when his calling was announced in church, one of the feelings I had was jealousy.

I hope you found both of these stories pathetic. You need to understand that I have the greatest job ever in human history—I get to talk about the arts with bright and curious young people. I live in a lovely home in a delightful neighborhood. I make more than enough money. So why would I feel jealousy? Because I compare myself to others—my daughter and her family and my colleague and new Bishop. I judge them and judge myself. I want hardwood floors. I don't want to be bishop, but Bishop is a sign of high status in my group. I can pretend that my feelings don't exist or that I'm not jealous or that I don't compare and judge, but that would be dishonest. I'm a member of a family, a ward, and society. My family, ward, and society use judgement and comparison to solve the free rider problem. Money and status are ways members measure their place and their value in the group, so when I see group members making more money and enjoying higher status, I judge and compare. When I have less, make less, or conclude that I have a lower status, I feel jealous.

A PRACTICAL RESPONSE TO THE DOUG DILEMMA IN THREE STEPS

I see three practical steps as a solution to my jealousy. These steps respond to the judgment, comparison, and trash talking that groups use to address the Doug Dilemma. All three steps start with "h." As you might have guessed, the last one is going to be humility, but we are going to build to that.

I know that when my loved ones read those two above stories, they will cringe. The stories are embarrassing, and they will feel embarrassed for me. My jealousy is petty and foolish. I hope that you find the stories a little absurd. Hopefully it doesn't make sense to you to care about how much money someone makes or what kind of possessions someone has. I really hope it doesn't make sense to see church callings as signs of status. Hopefully you don't picture wards like a pyramid with the Bishop and his counsellors on top and the ward counsel just below him, with the various organizations and members filling out the pyramid's middle and base. Hopefully you don't see stake, mission, or general church leadership like that—with highest leaders on top and lower status leaders arranged below them. Hopefully you never create any association between how valuable group members are and how high up they are. Hopefully you never feel like God's approval is sometimes vague and one's value to the church can also be hard to pin down. Hopefully you never view being assigned to a calling with a lot of responsibility as a sign of one's value to the group as well as an affirmation of God's approval and trust. I hope that none of that makes any sense to you.

I hope I'm the only one who falls into seeing my group in this way, but perhaps you do judge and compare members of your group. There are lots of ways to judge status, value, and reputation in a group, including praise, honor, and group benefits that higher status members enjoy. Still, perhaps none of this applies to you. But if you do happen to find yourself judging and comparing, the first practical solution I propose is honesty. Walking into my daughter's house and feeling jealous was very discouraging for me. I wanted to just be completely happy for them. In the moment, the jealousy wasn't the strongest feeling, so I didn't feel the need to hide it from my family. But as I reflected on the situation later, I saw that jealousy was one of my feelings.

I find it helpful to honestly recognize and acknowledge these petty, foolish feelings. It was helpful for me to name the feeling. Naming the feeling somehow makes it less overwhelming. Giving it a name makes that gloomy, cloudlike impression solidify into something I can get my mind around. Naming is part of honesty, at least for me, because I want to pretend those undesired feelings don't exist. I'm embarrassed for myself. I cringe at me. Honestly naming is an act of courage, at least for me.

It was also helpful to think about why I felt jealous. I recognized how successful my daughter and her husband have been. I compared their success to mine. In one marker of success and enjoying group benefits—making money—they are more valuable to the group than I am. Yes, I can complain about capitalism and markets and how income poorly equates to value, but those reasons cannot take away my feelings. I can say that church callings have little or nothing to do with righteousness or value in God's kingdom. Here again, those reasons don't take away the jealous feelings I had when I compared myself to the new bishop. As part of my groups, I judge and compare.

To illustrate the importance of being honest about my feelings and why it is valuable to frankly examine those feelings, I like the following analogy. My feelings are like a bomb. Those feelings are very powerful. My emotions motivate me. When I examine my feelings, it is like I'm defusing a bomb. I examine how the parts of the bomb work, how they are connected, what wires go to what parts. When I understand the bomb's mechanisms, I can cut the proper wires so it won't go off unexpectedly. I can also rewire the bomb in such a way that it works for me. I can even disassemble it and use its parts to make something more beneficial.

Honest examination seems like a better solution than pretending that the feelings are not there. It is also a better solution than trying to tell myself to not have those feelings. Finally, honesty is a better solution than pretending that I don't care about status or about feeling valued by my groups. Repeating to myself like a chant "how much money they make doesn't matter" or "your church calling doesn't matter" or "you just need to stop comparing and judging and feeling jealous" leaves me in the dark as to what is really going on inside of me. It leaves me in the dark with a bomb, it is a bomb that I don't understand, and all of my chanting, pretending, and avoiding cannot bring me to the light and to safety. If I acknowledge my feelings and then examine them, I can trace them back to judgement, comparison, trash talking, and the free rider problem. I can see how my feelings are natural outcomes of how groups discourage free riders and encourage full participation. Those feelings are not pleasant or desirable, but I can understand where they come from.

Honestly examining my feelings and connecting those feelings with the fact that I'm part of several group projects is my first practical solution. My second solution is something that C.S. Lewis suggested. In his book *The Screwtape Letters*, Lewis has one demon write to another about how to attack a person's humility. The demon points out that if people start to become humble, one solution is to point out that they are being humble. The goal is to make the person proud of being humble. Clever. But then the demon gives this warning: "Don't try this too long, for fear you awake his sense of humor and proportion, in which case he will merely laugh at you and go to bed." And that is my second solution—humor. Reflecting on my jealousy in my daughter's house and during the sacrament meeting when the new bishop was called gave me a chance to laughed at myself. I found humor in my pettiness and foolishness. Honesty helped me see those feelings and trace their source. Humor helped me laugh at the foolishness of a grown man jealous of his daughter and her family. I love my ward and our new bishop, and I realized that there I was, like a child seeing another kid get something that he doesn't even really want, but once someone else gets it, he whines, "I want some too." It was all so laughable.

Lewis' demon notes that what can come awake for us is a sense of humor and proportion. Honestly understanding and then laughing puts things in perspective. Laughter reduces something large and overwhelming to its truer size and importance. Understanding and laughing at my jealousy gave me a bit of space between myself and my emotional response. Understanding and laughing made it easier to be patient with myself and to focus on the other feelings that were also present.

Focusing on the other feelings that were present leads to the third practical solution—humility. After I'm honest about my feelings and the situation, and after I gain some delightful space and perspective through laughter and humor, I can refocus my attention. I can remind myself that my Heavenly Parents are the Lord my God. I can be submissive, committed, and devoted to Them. God has given me a work to do. Part of that work is loving and serving the people around me. I get to do my part in the group project that is God's kingdom on the earth. I can remember the intimate friendship with God that I can enjoy as I do my part. I can also remind myself that my pettiness and foolishness are part of the weakness God gives me. They are part of my Penia or poverty. I recall how God can fill this need or lack with the rich Poros of God's grace. This recollection fills me with purpose and joy.

In addition to reminding myself that I'm God's child with a work to do in God's kingdom, I can refocus on my relationships with those around me. I remember my loving commitment to them. My love and my relationships with others teach me how to be the best friend possible. I can remind myself that others are a mystery to me. I can never know who they really are and what they are going through. My judgements are always incomplete and deeply flawed. Finally, those around me don't need my judgements; they do need my compassion.

TWO NIGHT SKY ANALOGIES

To appreciate the value of honesty, humor, and humility, here are two night sky analogies. Analogy number one: in Dante's *Divine Comedy*, the poet describes being lifted up into heaven. As he rises higher and higher, he looks down between his feet. From these lofty heights, earth seems small and pathetic. That is what humility does for me. I acknowledge my unpleasant and undesired feelings. I trace their source to the nasty, brutish reality of trash talking in groups. I laugh at my foolishness and pettiness. I humbly shift my focus to my relationship with God and the work God has for me. That humble shift lifts me from a dark dreariness and pettiness into light, life, and purpose. All my jealousy, judgment, and comparison become small and pathetic.

Analogy number two: I have a vivid memory of riding in the family station wagon as a kid from Virginia to Utah. One night as we made our way through Wyoming, I recall looking at a night sky dripping with stars. I felt a deep sense of awe at the sight. I also noticed that it seemed like I could see more stars in my peripheral vision than when I looked right at them. Later I learned that it is the structure of the eye that makes stars easier to see with one's peripheral vision. Next time you are out and want to see a faint star, try focusing away from it. Notice how you see faint stars more clearly by not looking directly at them. When I humbly shift my focus to my relationship with God and the work God has for me, especially how God can bless others through me, I stop looking exclusively on myself. The humble shift helps me see God and others better. And once I stop trying to look at myself and instead focus on God and others, I actually see myself better. I see my place, my role, and my most important relationships and work. This humble refocus is not an effort to stop thinking about me. It is the work of focusing on God, God's work for me, and my relationships with others. I don't think less about myself. For me, telling myself to think less about me doesn't seem to work. I humbly redirect my focus and what happens is I get a better, more truthful, and more reliable understanding of myself thrown in.

Humility connects me with God, with others, and with a truer and more reliable understanding of myself and my place in this group project. Humility puts everything in its right place. It is wonderful. It is also, at least for me, temporary. Humility puts things in their right place, but in my experience, things always end up getting scrambled again. I cannot seem to remain in the heaven of full light, complete life, and unwavering purpose. I always fall back to earth. I will find myself judging and comparing and competing, feeling envious and jealous and inadequate, and falling into the same pettiness and foolishness. I used to think that time, maturity, repentance, and obedience could make me pure enough in heart that I would never fall back into trash talking, judgement, and comparison. Perhaps some people achieve that. My experience is that life is a constant moving back and forth between being a worker in God's vineyard with divine purpose and celestial perspective and being a trash talking mastodon hunter or a lazy Doug promising to catch up with the group after a brief "self-care" power nap. Humility lifts me into the Poros of God's grace, but I always fall back into the Penia of mortality, judgment, and comparison. Perhaps that constant interplay between Penia and Poros is what I need so that I can become what God wants me to become.

The back-and-forth of humility's heavenly perspective and natural man judgment and comparison helps me grow and develop into a celestial being. The Penia of my weakness comes together with the Poros of God's grace to change and transform me. I develop qualities and skills that make me more fluent. I'm always somewhere in the middle of this process. I'm normal. The book's concluding chapter explores what it means to be normal.

CONCLUSION:
THE JOY OF BEING NORMAL

One last point and the book is done: you and I are normal. Yes we are proud, we judge, and we compare. We come up short in our complete devotion to God. We are not quite the friend or equal partner or follower or leader that we could be. That, in my opinion, is normal. Like everyone else, there are times when we could really use a good parent, a good teacher, coach or boss. A good therapist, good leaders, and great friends are also wonderful! That's okay. That's to be expected. We are normal.

There is another reason we are normal. That reason is that, sadly, any Miss Brodies in our lives may have tried to convince us that we were special. Maybe we believed them. They flattered us and appealed to our pride to get us to do good things. They told us that breaking commandments is beneath us. Breaking those commandments is something "other people" do. This led us to look down on others. Sometimes we have used our righteousness to measure and to judge others. The reality is that our obedience does not make us special. In fact, no righteousness makes us special. We are not the "crème de la crème." Instead of being special, what we really are is normal.

Since we are normal, we are just like everyone else. And just like everyone else, each of us has a unique work to do. God wants to co-operate with you in blessing the lives of people around you. Others will miss blessings God wants to give them if you are not there. Like everyone else, you spend your life trying to figure out what that work is, understand that work, and developing the skills and fluencies so that you can do God's work to the best of your ability. As you try to do God's work to the best of your ability, you find those efforts deeply satisfying and exhilarating. There are times when you feel a wonderful enthusiasm. I'm using the word "enthusiasm" for a specific reason. At its root, the word "enthusiasm" means "God inside of you." There are times when you do your best to bring all of your skills together with God's matchless grace and power to bless the lives of the people you love. This activity fills you with joy, with a sense of awe, and with a sense of reverence for the privilege of co-operating with God. These are times when it feels like God is inside of you.

And there is one last way that you and I are normal. Okay, maybe we are not special. We are not royalty, and we were not generals in the spiritual war before we came to earth. In God's view, no one has any status above or below any of God's other children. No job or education or accomplishment or possessions or tax bracket or church calling makes anyone special. When we want to remember who we really are and what it means to be a normal, regular person, we remember this: had you been the only person that needed saving, Christ still would have done everything He did. Even if it were just for you, Christ would have come down from heaven, subjected Himself to mortality, revealed the path back to God, suffered and passed beneath your worst and most painful experiences, agonized in Gethsemane and on the cross, and resurrected. That is what Christ did for you. That is what Christ did for every regular, normal person. Each person in your life—your spouse, friends, children, parents, co-workers, teammates, therapist, leaders, all of the people you see in church, the hospital pharmacist, the dear friend with dark seasons of depression, the still-grieving widow, the flight attendant, the struggling student, the data analytics specialist at the large company, the taxi driver, the human resources person, the new mom, the new dad, the new bishop, the customer service representatives on the other side of the phone or the email conversation, the middle school history teacher, the discouraged missionary, the Relief Society president, the crazy man singing his heart out in his car at the stoplight—Christ did all He did for every one of these regular, normal people. Christ's sacrifice, His infinite Atonement, tells you that you are just like everyone else and that each one of us is an infinitely valuable child of loving Heavenly Parents. Those Parents invite you to be a full participant in the group project that is preparing all of us to live with Them and be like Them forever. This is what it means to be normal. This is what it means to be you.

NOTES

Welcome to the notes! These notes provide some useful background knowledge for those interested in the topic and specify where the citations come from. For anyone interested in humility, perhaps your best first LDS source is, of course, the humility topic essay. This essay has an overview as well as scriptures and talks about the topic. These are excellent online resources. When I last checked this, I noticed that one remarkable discussion of humility is not there. That discussion is a talk about humility by Spencer W. Kimball, a member of the Quorum of the Twelve Apostles at the time, given at BYU as a devotional on January 16, 1963. Another important touchstone talk, one that is included in the gospel topic essay on pride, is President Benson's very famous talk "Beware of Pride" delivered in the April 1989 General Conference.

If you are interested in how other Christians have spoken insightfully about humility, one of the most insightful and commonly talked about sources is C.S. Lewis' chapter about pride, a chapter called "The Great Sin," in his book *Mere Christianity*. This book was first published in 1952, but has since been republished many times. This is chapter nine from the book's third section. Another very often cited source is Andrew Murray's book *Humility: The Journey Toward Holiness*. Murray was born in the 1800s, and this book has also been republished many times. Murray emphasizes humility as complete dependence upon God. A current, academic book about humility (and pride) that brings together a lot of current thinking about the topic is *Pride and Humility: A New Interdisciplinary Analysis*. This was published by Palgrave in 2016. The book brings together scholarship from the social sciences and the humanities, and, though I admit to having mixed feelings about the author, it is an insightful examination.

INTRODUCTION

* These quotes from Chinua Achebe's *Things Fall Apart* are found in the last paragraph of the book's sixteenth chapter.

* The idea that you are becoming complete, whole, and fully formed into the person God wants you to be is a very important idea. This idea is perhaps best explained in President Nelson's October 1995 General Conference address "Perfection Pending." President Nelson explains how "perfect," when it is used in Matthew 5:48, is better understood as complete, fully developed, or achieving a distant goal rather than flawless.

The last sentence of the introduction puts forward that, "This
study can lead you to the gracious gift of God's rain." To the
degree that humility toward God is complete submission, commitment, and devotion to God, the study of humility can also
lead us to the gracious gift of God's complete sovereignty and
"reign." Hehehe.

ONE   YOU ARE THE LORD MY GOD

I am grateful to Jerilyn Hassell Pool for her willingness to
share her experiences with me. This account is shared with her
permission.

If you are interested in the idea of humility as believing in something that seems too good to be true, another vivid description
comes from the Danish thinker Søren Kierkegaard. In his book
The Sickness Unto Death, Kierkegaard imagines a poor day laborer
who lives in a country with a mighty emperor. The day laborer
is so distant from the emperor that he cannot imagine that the
emperor has any idea who he is. If this lowly worker had the
chance to see the emperor even once, according to Kierkegaard,
it would be the sort of hugely important, remarkable day that
the laborer would probably tell his children and grandchildren
about. But Kierkegaard throws in a curve ball. He asks how this
worker might feel if the emperor not only wanted to meet with
him, but what if the emperor wanted this worker to be a family
member? What if, for example, the emperor wanted the laborer

to marry one of his daughters and become the emperor's son-in-law? Kierkegaard says that the worker would probably feel puzzled, self-conscious, and embarrassed by this proposition. He would probably conclude that the emperor was trying to make a fool of him. This situation would seem so strange and so bizarre that the worker would either try to hide the invitation or even feel offended by it. Kierkegaard says that the worker would say something like "Such a thing is too high for me, I cannot grasp it; to be perfectly blunt, to me it is a piece of folly."

After talking about his day worker and his invitation to not only meet the emperor but to marry his daughter, Kierkegaard makes this amazing comparison:

> And now, what of Christianity! Christianity teaches that this individual human being—and thus every single individual human being, no matter whether man, woman, servant, girl, cabinet minister, merchant, barber, student, or whatever—this individual human being exists *before God*, this individual human being who perhaps would be proud of having spoken with the king once in his life, this human being who does not have the slightest illusion of being on intimate terms with this one or that one, this human being exists before God, may speak with God any time he wants to, assured of being heard by

him—in short, this person is invited to live on the most intimate terms with God!

The person who would be almost overwhelmed to be an emperor's son-in-law can actually be on intimate terms with God. Kierkegaard goes on:

> Furthermore, for this person's sake, also for this very person's sake, God comes to the world, allows himself to be born, to suffer, to die, and this suffering God—he almost implores and beseeches this person to accept the help that is offered to him! Truly, if there is anything to lose one's mind over, this is it!

Kierkegaard elaborates that God not only invites you to have a relationship with God, but God even comes into mortality, suffers, and dies for you. And then Kierkegaard makes this conclusion: "Everyone lacking the humble courage to dare to believe this is offended." When you think about humility as believing God when something God promises and reveals seems too good to be true, Kierkegaard reminds you that it requires humility to risk what might seem like the foolishness of believing God. This analogy shows how humility, courage, and faith work together. The above story and quotes are from pages 84 and 85 of the Howard V. and Edna H. Hong translation of *The Sickness Unto Death*, published by Princeton University Press in 1980.

*   "Marty" is a pseudonym. His story is used by permission.

*   Brett Scharffs' experience is found in his 2005 BYU devotional "The Most Important Three Things in the World."

*   Two final notes should be added to this chapter. Besides the four aspects of humility in your relationship with God described in this chapter, there are two more that should be mentioned. The first aspect is humility as total dependence on God. The wonderful church hymn "I Need Thee Every Hour" expresses this notion beautifully. Humility as acknowledging total dependence on God is also an excellent antidote to the arrogance of believing that you don't need God.

    A second aspect of humility is self-forgetfulness. C.S. Lewis, in *Mere Christianity*, illustrates this idea of humility about forgetting about yourself when he says,

> Do not imagine that if you meet a really humble man he will be what most people call 'humble' nowadays: he will not be a sort of greasy, smarmy person, who is always telling you that, of course, he is nobody. Probably all you will think about him is that he seemed a cheerful, intelligent chap who took a real interest in what you said to him. If you do dislike him it will be because you feel a little envious of anyone who seems to enjoy life

so easily. He will not be thinking about humility: he will not be thinking about himself at all.

This last line shows how, in Lewis' view, humility means thinking about God or thinking about the people you are with from moment-to-moment but not thinking about yourself. A single example of these two ideas about humility—complete dependence on God and self-forgetfulness—is special moments of prayer or of giving a blessing. You may have had the experience of praying or giving a blessing where you feel that the words simply flowed through you to others. You may have felt that the words were given to you, and you were merely the voice. You took a backseat or you disappeared, so to speak, as the Lord's will was made manifest. To put it another way, you became more and more transparent as the face and will of God became more obvious, visible, and apparent. Moments like this are powerful, unforgettable, and transcendent.

I did not address humility as complete dependence on God and as self-forgetfulness in this section for a couple of reasons. One reason is that I am not trying to say everything that there is to say about humility. My goal is to speak insightfully about some elements of humility. I trust the reader will fill in some of the gaps with their own insights and experiences. Another reason is that the four aspects I did address seemed to be enough. Two more, it seemed to me, made it seem unwieldy and a bit overwhelming.

But a deeper reason for choosing to not include dependence and self-forgetfulness in this chapter comes from an experience I had at an academic conference. One of the presenters talked at length about humility. His focus was humility as dependence and self-forgetfulness. After his presentation, a woman approached the presenter, thanked him for his presentation, but then expressed a concern. Her concern, which she stated with respect and kindness, was that in her experience humility as dependence and self-forgetfulness were too often overemphasized. Besides being overemphasized, she pointed out that women, minorities, and other disempowered peoples too often embrace humility as being dependent and self-forgetful but miss some of humility's other aspects. This overemphasis unfortunately gives, in her view, disempowered people the false idea that being dependent and self-forgetful is always a good thing and something to be very strongly encouraged. Overemphasizing these elements of humility discourages people from bravely trusting God and moving forward with faith and power to positively impact the world around them. Since I think dependence and self-forgetfulness are already commonplace ideas in discussions of humility, and since I think that the Penia and Poros discussion as well as the second night sky analogy cover these areas well enough, I did not want to further reinforce and risk overemphasizing them in this chapter.

TWO HUMILITY'S FOUNDATION, OR A TALE OF A WHALE AND FRIENDSHIP

The quotes from Melville's *Moby Dick* are from the book's 103rd ✱ chapter "Measurement of The Whale's Skeleton." They are in the ninth paragraph in that chapter.

The discussion of *Moby Dick* is inspired by Northrop Frye's writ- ✱ ing, specifically his *Anatomy of Criticism: Four Essays*, published by Princeton University Press in 1957. In this book Frye says that *Moby Dick* has elements of an "anatomy." For Frye an anatomy is a dissection or an analysis of intellectual patterns. One such pattern is the encyclopedia. Frye makes the case that Melville makes fun or satirizes that approach. He makes this argument on pages 308 through 313. Jed Rasula, in the article *Textual Indigence in the Archive*, expands and refines this insight. Rasula's article was published in *Postmodern Culture*, volume 9, number 3, in May of 1999.

Elder Boyd K. Packer's talk "The Touch of the Master's Hand" ✱ was given in the April 2001 General Conference.

President Benson quotes C.S. Lewis in his April 1989 General ✱ Conference talk "Beware of Pride." This is in the tenth paragraph of President Benson's talk. C.S. Lewis' statement about pride and enmity is in the fifth paragraph of his chapter "The Great Sin" in his book *Mere Christianity*.

* One quote from the prophet Joseph Smith reinforces this chapter's point about friendship. On page 316 of the *Teachings of the Prophet Joseph Smith*, the prophet says that "Friendship is one of the grand fundamental principles of "Mormonism"; [it is designed] to revolutionize and civilize the world, and cause wars and contentions to cease and men to become friends and brothers."

THREE   COMPLEMENTS, PARTNERS, AND FLUENT MISSIONARIES

* The story of Poros and Penia is found in Plato's *Symposium*. It is part of Socrates' discussion of the nature of love.

* I use the story of Poros and Penia to describe a humble desire to learn and grow. Another, more current way to describe this desire to learn and grow is Dr. Carol Dweck's insights about the growth mindset. In her book *Mindset: The New Psychology of Success*, published by Ballantine in several editions, including a 2007 updated edition, Dr. Dweck describes the "growth mindset" as being eager to learn, eager to acquire new skills, a willingness to put forth effort, and the ability to overcome setbacks and readily accept feedback. Dweck contrasts this approach with a "fixed mindset" wherein one believes that skills, intellect, and talents are inborn and unchangeable. What follows from such a fixed mindset is an unwillingness to learn or attempt to acquire new skills, an unwillingness to put forward effort, and an inability to overcome setbacks or accept feedback. Dweck's "growth

mindset" is an excellent expression for humility as the desire to learn and develop.

One inspiration for this discussion of vulnerability is Brené   ✳
Brown's insights about this topic. Her most famous discussion is
her 2010 TED talk "The Power of Vulnerability."

FOUR KENT, CORDELIA, AND MARTY'S FRIENDS

Lear's discussions with his daughters, rejection of Cordelia, and   ✳
expulsion of Kent all take place in Act 1, scene 1 of Shakespeare's
play. Lear's line about the bow being bent is line 144. Kent's reply
is lines 145–155. Lear responds in line 156 and then Kent in lines
157–59. Lear tells Kent to get out of his sight in line 160, and Kent
replies "see better" in line 161. Lear's accusations are lines 172–84.
Cordelia's lines about loving according to her bond is in line 93.

Cordelia's reconciliation with her father is in Act 4, scene 7.
Cordelia asks her father to "look upon me, sir" in line 58. Lear
responds in lines 61–72. Cordelia reassures him in line 73, to
which Lear responds about her tears being wet in line 74. He talks
about poison and her sisters in lines 75–77, and she responds "no
cause, no cause" in line 78.

Emily Dickinson wrote a really wonderful poem about helping   ✳
people see the truth in a way that gently invites them to see it.
The poem has the first line, "Tell all the truth but tell it slant—."

FIVE HUMILITY IN RELATIONSHIPS WITH EQUALS, OR WHY JANE CAN'T FIND THE MEDIUM

* Jane's line that "I never in my life have known any medium" is found in chapter 34 of *Jane Eyre*. It is found toward the middle of the chapter. The paragraph reads:

> I know no medium: I never in my life have known any medium in my dealings with positive, hard characters, antagonistic to my own, between absolute submission and determined revolt. I have always faithfully observed the one, up to the very moment of bursting, sometimes with volcanic vehemence, into the other; and as neither present circumstances warranted, nor my present mood inclined me to mutiny, I observed careful obedience to St. John's directions; and in ten minutes I was treading the wild track of the glen, side by side with him.

Jane describes herself as a "rebel slave" in chapter 2's first paragraph. It reads:

> I resisted all the way: a new thing for me, and a circumstance which greatly strengthened the bad opinion Bessie and Miss Abbot were disposed to entertain of me. The fact is, I was a

trifle beside myself; or rather out of myself, as the French would say: I was conscious that a moment's mutiny had already rendered me liable to strange penalties, and, like any other rebel slave, I felt resolved, in my desperation, to go all lengths.

Jane's assertion to Rochester that she be her equal comes in chapter 23. She puts it this way:

"I tell you I must go!" I retorted, roused to something like passion. "Do you think I can stay to become nothing to you? Do you think I am an automaton?—a machine without feelings? and can bear to have my morsel of bread snatched from my lips, and my drop of living water dashed from my cup? Do you think, because I am poor, obscure, plain, and little, I am soulless and heartless? You think wrong!—I have as much soul as you,—and full as much heart! And if God had gifted me with some beauty and much wealth, I should have made it as hard for you to leave me, as it is now for me to leave you. I am not talking to you now through the medium of custom, conventionalities, nor even of mortal flesh;—it is my spirit that addresses your spirit; just as if both had passed through the grave, and we stood at God's feet, equal,—as we are!"

* The complete title for John Lund's book is *For All Eternity: Practical Tools for Strengthening Your Marriage*. The book's 2014 publisher was Covenant Communications. Dr. Lund's insights about the language of request and respect are found in chapter four. From the standpoint of respectful and humble interaction with equals, the book provides excellent insights.

* I acknowledge here that the discussion about how a married Jane might have to faithfully and humbly struggle to establish a truly equal relationship with St. John is inspired by ideas I have heard from Dr. Jennifer Finlayson-Fife.

* Dickens's line about how others are a profound secret and mystery to us is the first sentence of the third chapter of his book *A Tale of Two Cities*. That chapter has the title, "The Night Shadows."

SIX   HUMILITY IN UNEQUAL RELATIONSHIPS

* The Phoebus cartel is described in Wyatt Well's 2002 book *Antitrust and the Formation of the Postwar World*. It is discussed on pages 20–22, and this book was published by Columbia University press. Other sources include Markus Krajewski's article "The Great Lightbulb Conspiracy," published in IEEE *Spectrum* on September 24, 2014.

My discussion of Professor Mike Sanford's approach to teaching   ✳
art is published with his permission.

The quotes from M. Scott Peck's book *The Road Less Travelled* are   ✳
from pages 154–55. Peck's book was first published by Simon &
Schuster in 1978.

The quotes from Brigham Young are taken from page 150 of the   ✳
Journal of Discourses, volume 9.

SEVEN USING SATAN'S TOOLS TO DO GOD'S WORK

The Dementors act as guards at Azkaban prison in J.K. Rowling's   ✳
novel *Harry Potter and the Prisoner of Azkaban*. They join Voldemort
in *Harry Potter and the Order of the Phoenix*. Voldemort calls the
Dementors his natural allies in *Harry Potter and the Goblet of Fire*,
Chapter 33, "The Death Eaters."

The *Missionary Guide* section cited here, the section called   ✳
"Asking Appropriate Questions," is on pages 111–13. The manipulative sample discussion about tithing is found on page 131. At
the time of this writing, the *Missionary Guide* can be found at
archive.org.

* The quote from Muriel Spark's novel *The Prime of Miss Jean Brodie* about "life's élite" is on page 36 of the novel. The quotes about her "new pupils" and feeling "chosen" are on page 116.

* The quotes from Lewis' *Mere Christianity* about pride beating "down the simpler vices," overcoming "cowardice, or lust or ill-temper," and setting up "the Dictatorship of Pride" are found in the chapter's eighth paragraph. The paragraph also contains Lewis' assertion that pride "eats up the very possibility of love." Lewis, speaking of Satan and pride, says "just as he would be quite content to see your chilblains cured if he was allowed, in return, to give you cancer." I used acne instead of "chilblains" because I'm guessing that my audience is just as unfamiliar with chilblains as I was. I think my substitution retains the spirit of Lewis' comparison while making it easier for the reader to understand.

* The sample manipulative questions from the *Missionary Guide* are found on pages 111 and 113.

* Elder Neal Maxwell's BYU devotional has the title "Patience," and it was given on November 27, 1979. The quote is in the 28th paragraph.

* Paul telling Timothy that God has not given us the "spirit of fear" is found in 2nd Timothy 1:7.

EIGHT HUMILITY IN TALKING ABOUT POLITICS

On June 24, 2015, Carly Ledbetter published an article in the Life   ✸
section of Huffpost with the title "Science Explains Why Cilantro
Tastes Like Soap For Certain People." The article describes sci-
entific research into why some people do not like cilantro.

Jonathan Haidt's ideas about the five parts of morality and how   ✸
"liberals" and "conservatives" experience or "taste" morality
differently are found in his book *The Righteous Mind: Why Good
People Are Divided by Politics and Religion*. It was published by
Vintage in 2012. My discussion comes from the book's second
section, "There's More to Morality than Harm and Fairness."
I will say that Haidt's ideas seem useful and valid, but, like all
knowledge, they have their limitations. In addition, one would
anticipate that Haidt's insights will be modified, expanded, and
challenged both now and in the future. I'm not using Haidt's
insights because they are eternally "true" or are permanent
and flawless. I'm using them to illustrate how good, moral people can see the world differently. I'm using them to show how
such differences can be respected and valued. Other current
thinkers also describe how "liberals" and "conservatives" see
the world and morality. George Lakoff's book *The All New Don't
Think of an Elephant! Know Your Values and Frame the Debate* also
describes liberal and conservative ways of seeing the world. I
mention Lakoff's book to illustrate how people are attempting

to understand liberal and conservative points-of-view. I chose to use Haidt's version because it seems even-handed and respectful.

* Robert S. Wood's April, 2006 General Conference talk is "Instruments of the Lord's Peace."

ELEVEN PRACTICAL HUMILITY IN DAILY LIFE AND THE JOY OF BEING NORMAL

* I'm only dealing with a very small sliver of the free rider problem. Some of the most influential scholarship that explores the social psychological elements of this problem includes Ernst Fehr and Simon Gächter's article "Altruistic Punishment in Humans," (*Nature* 415, 137–140, https://doi.org/10.1038/415137a) as well as "Egalitarian Motive and Altruistic Punishment" by James H. Fowler, Tim Johnson and Oleg Smirnov (*Nature* 433, E1, https://doi.org/10.1038/nature03256). "The Rise and Fall of Cooperation Through Reputation and Group Polarization" by Jörg Gross and Carsten K. W. De Dreu (*Nature Communications* 10, 776, https://doi.org/10.1038/s41467-019-08727-8) is a recent exploration of cooperation and reputation as they apply to the free rider problem. For an insightful and related discussion, see Alain de Botton's *Status Anxiety* published by Penguin in 2004.

* There is a phrase I have heard among members of the church that illustrates judgment, trash talking, and reputation in the church. The numbers fluctuate, but the phrase is "15% of the

ward members to 80% of the work." If you have heard any variation on this, you have heard members trash talking in just the ways I have described.

This is a rather long (but worthwhile) note about the value of naming. In Yan Martel's book *Life of Pi*, the narrator, who is stuck on a boat with a tiger, speaks insightfully about fear. I will quote this at some length because of what he says about the value of naming fear and what happens when we don't name such feelings.

> I must say a word about fear. It is life's only true opponent. Only fear can defeat life. It is a clever, treacherous adversary, how well I know. It has no decency, respects no law or convention, shows no mercy. It goes for your weakest spot, which it finds with unerring ease. It begins in your mind, always. One moment you are feeling calm, self-possessed, happy. Then fear, disguised in the garb of mild-mannered doubt, slips into your mind like a spy. Doubt meets disbelief and disbelief tries to push it out. But disbelief is a poorly armed foot soldier. Doubt does away with it with little trouble. You become anxious. Reason comes to do battle for you. You are reassured. Reason is fully equipped with the latest weapons technology. But, to your amazement, despite superior tactics and a number of undeniable victories,

reason is laid low. You feel yourself weakening, wavering. Your anxiety becomes dread.

Fear next turns fully to your body, which is already aware that something terribly wrong is going on. Already your lungs have flown away like a bird and your guts have slithered away like a snake. Now your tongue drops dead like an opossum, while your jaw begins to gallop on the spot. Your ears go deaf. Your muscles begin to shiver as if they had malaria and your knees to shake as though they were dancing. Your heart strains too hard, while your sphincter relaxes too much. And so with the rest of your body. Every part of you, in the manner most suited to it, falls apart. Only your eyes work well. They always pay proper attention to fear.

Quickly you make rash decisions. You dismiss your last allies: hope and trust. There, you've defeated yourself. Fear, which is but an impression, has triumphed over you.

The matter is difficult to put into words. For fear, real fear, such as shakes you to your foundation, such as you feel when you are brought face to face with your mortal end, nestles in your memory like a gangrene: it seeks to rot everything, even the words with which to speak of it. So you must fight hard to express it. You must fight hard to shine the light of words upon it. Because if you don't, if your fear becomes a wordless darkness that you avoid, perhaps even manage to forget, you open yourself to further attacks of fear because you never truly fought the opponent who defeated you. (Yann Martel *Life of Pi* page 161)

The section where the demon warns the other about how humor ✳ and laughter might subvert their efforts in C.S. Lewis' *The Screwtape Letters* is found on pages 69-70. This quote as well as other ideas about laughter's place in LDS culture are addressed in "On Mormon Laughter" (BYU *Studies Quarterly* 51.4 pp. 141–154). This is a fair article overall, though I must admit to rather mixed feelings about the study's author.

With regards to step two—I'm also aware that not everyone ✳ finds humor to be as useful as I do. Not everyone is a jokester. If you are not a jokester, gratitude seems to offer similar distance and perspective.

Dante's experience of rising into heaven and looking down at ✳ earth is described in the last portion of Canto 22 in the *Paradise* portion of his *Divine Comedy*. John Ciardi's translation is: "My eyes went back through the seven spheres below, / and I saw this globe, so small, so lost in space, / I had to smile at such a sorry show" (Canto 20, lines 133–35).

* The chapter doesn't state this outright, but what it proposes is a unique solution to the free rider problem. That solution is God. If I believe that God is watching me and that God holds me accountable for my part in the group project, then I'm motivated to not free ride. In fact, I'm motivated to contribute with my whole heart, might, mind, and strength. My contributions thus linked to God can sanctify them. In contributing and working, I work for God. I can enjoy all of the benefits that that work can provide. I can rely on God to judge me. If I can measure God's judgement successfully, I may feel less anxiety about both judging myself and judging others. In addition, it is easier to acknowledge that others are a mystery to me because only God knows and properly judges me, and I assume the same for others. Still, God as a solution to the free rider problem only works if humility is a key element of one's relationship with God and if humility typifies one's relationships with others. God and humility as a solution seem particularly divine when that solution is contrasted with the earthy, brutal, and anxiety-ridden solution of trash talking, comparing, and judging.

INDEX

ACKNOWLEDGMENTS

I'm so grateful for everyone at By Common Consent Press for their professionalism, patience, and diligence in bringing this project to fruition. Specifically, thanks to Michael Austin, Andrew Heiss, Christian Harrison, and Shannyn Thompson Walters for your efforts. I'm also grateful for the many missionaries who I conned into reading portions of the manuscript.

SHAWN TUCKER teaches Humanities at Elon University in Elon, North Carolina. In 2010, he received a National Endowment for the Humanities grant to develop a college course about Pride, Humility, and the Good Life. In 2016, he published *Pride and Humility: A New Interdisciplinary Analysis*, which is an academic examination of the topic. While on her mission, one of Shawn's daughters was foolish enough to ask for his ideas about humility. Nine letters later, Shawn had the basis for a book that brings together insights from his courses and his research on humility to offer something that might be useful for members of the Church of Jesus Christ of Latter-day Saints. That is this book. Shawn and his wife Nicole's four children have all grown up and they are currently saving China. Okay, not saving China (that was a *Mulan* reference), but they are living great lives. Shawn does not like cilantro, and his wife is always on the lookout for him trying to sneak a huge foam finger into sacrament meeting. Finally, Shawn would like to apologize to all of the Dougs of the world for making them a hiss and a byword.

Made in the USA
Monee, IL
26 January 2024